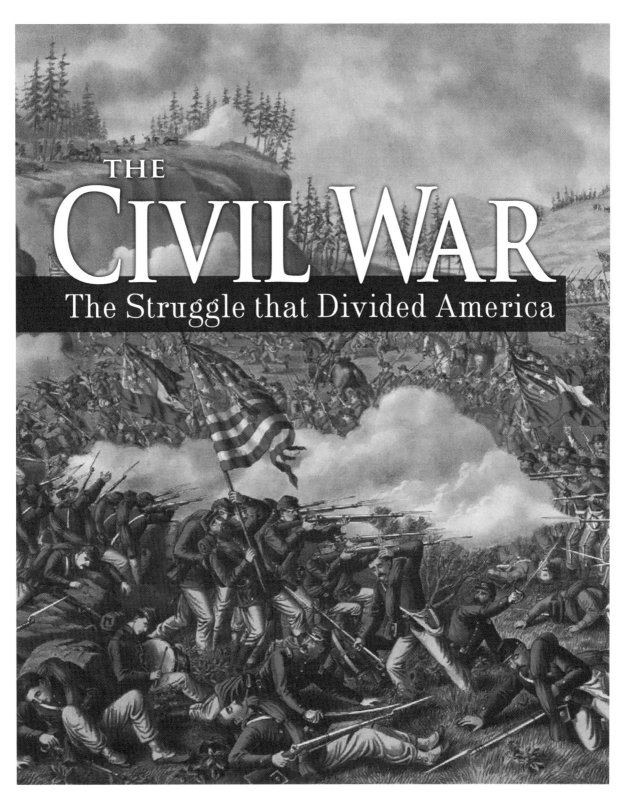

THE CIVIL WAR

The Struggle that Divided America

Judy Dodge Cummings
Illustrated by Sam Carbaugh

Nomad Press
A division of Nomad Communications
10 9 8 7 6 5 4 3 2 1

This book was manufactured by Versa Press
East Peoria, Illinois
November 2017, Job # J17-08785

ISBN Softcover: 978-1-61930-606-6
ISBN Hardcover: 978-1-61930-602-8

Educational Consultant, Marla Conn

Questions regarding the ordering of this book should be addressed to
Nomad Press
2456 Christian St.
White River Junction, VT 05001
www.nomadpress.net

Printed in the United States.

More social studies titles in the
Inquire and Investigate series

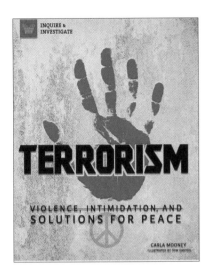

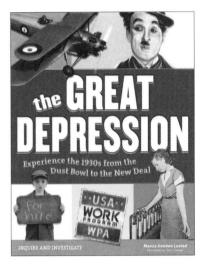

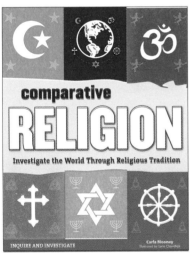

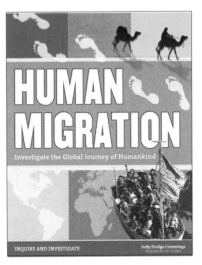

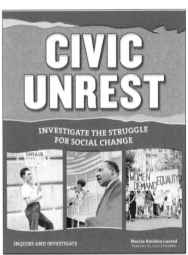

You can use a smartphone or tablet app to scan the QR codes and explore more! Cover up neighboring QR codes to make sure you're scanning the right one. You can find a list of URLs on the Resources page.

If the QR code doesn't work, try searching the Internet with the Keyword Prompts to find other helpful sources.

🔍 Civil War

Interested in primary sources? **Look for this icon.**

What are source notes?

In this book, you'll find small numbers at the end of some paragraphs. These numbers indicate that you can find source notes for that section in the back of the book. Source notes tell readers where the writer got their information. This might be a news article, a book, or another kind of media. Source notes are a way to know that what you are reading is true information that other people have verified. They can also lead you to more places where you can explore a topic that you're curious about!

Contents

TIMELINE

1619 .... The first African slaves arrive in Jamestown, Virginia.

1787 .... The United States Constitution is written, guaranteeing protections for slave owners.

1820 .... The Missouri Compromise becomes law in an attempt to balance the power between slave states and free states.

1833 .... The American Antislavery Society is established by abolitionists committed to ending slavery.

1846–1848 .... The United States fights a war with Mexico and wins extensive territory in the South and West.

1850 .... The Fugitive Slave Law is passed in another attempt to pacify Southern states, but the harsh law angers citizens in free states.

May 30, 1854 .... The Kansas-Nebraska Act is passed, permitting these territories to vote on whether they want slavery or not. Two years later, Kansas explodes in violence between proponents and opponents of slavery.

May 6, 1857 .... In the Dred Scott Decision, the U.S. Supreme Court rules that even free African Americans are not citizens and the government cannot restrict slave owners' right to take their slaves into free states.

October 16, 1859 .... Radical abolitionist John Brown raids the armory in Harper's Ferry, Virginia, in an effort to launch a slave rebellion.

November 6, 1860 .... Abraham Lincoln is elected president of the United States.

December 20, 1860 .... South Carolina is the first state to secede from the Union.

February 4, 1861 .... The Confederate States of America is formed.

April 12, 1861 .... The opening shots of the Civil War are fired when Confederate artillery bombs Fort Sumter.

TIMELINE

July 21, 1861 .... The First Battle of Bull Run occurs near Manassas, Virginia—this is the first major engagement of the Civil War.

April 6–7, 1862 .... The Battle of Shiloh in Tennessee results in more casualties than in all American wars combined up to this point.

September 17, 1862 .... The Battle of Antietam takes place in Sharpsburg, Maryland—this is the bloodiest day in American history.

January 1, 1863 .... President Lincoln signs the Emancipation Proclamation, freeing slaves in rebelling states and permitting African Americans to join the military.

July 1–3, 1863 .... The Battle of Gettysburg, in Pennsylvania, General Lee's second and last attempt to invade the North, fails.

May 18–July 4, 1863 .... The Union siege of Vicksburg, Mississippi, ends in victory, giving the Union control of the Mississippi River.

July 11–13, 1863 .... People in New York City riot over the draft.

November 15–December 21, 1864 ..... General Sherman leads the Union army on a destructive march from Atlanta, Georgia, to Savannah, Georgia.

March 4, 1865 .... President Lincoln is inaugurated into office for a second term.

April 9, 1865 .... General Lee surrenders to General Grant at the Appomattox Court House in Appomattox, Virginia, signaling the Civil War is all but over.

April 14, 1865 .... President Lincoln is shot while attending a play at Ford's Theater in Washington, DC.

April 15, 1865 .... Abraham Lincoln dies. Vice President Andrew Johnson is sworn in as president.

1865–1877 .... The period known as Reconstruction works to bring the former Confederate states back into the Union and establish basic rights for former slaves.

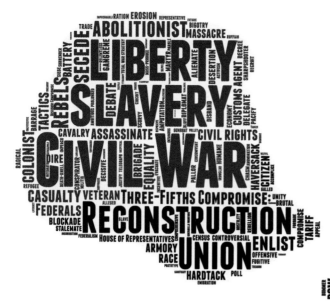

Introduction ▶

What Was the Civil War?

Why did the South decide to secede from the North and form the Confederacy?

Many different factors were part of the South's decision to secede from the United States, but the main issue that drove a wedge between the two sides was slavery.

Slavery or freedom? The question of whether to keep the United States a slave country or to grant freedom to all people was the issue that pitted the states against each other in a brutal conflict called the Civil War. This war raged from 1861 to 1865 and left more than 700,000 soldiers dead.

Why did the United States go to war with itself? What was at stake? Was the result of the conflict worth the horrific bloodshed? The buildup to the Civil War was a long one, beginning with the arrival of a slave ship in Virginia in 1619. However, the first official shots of the war were fired on a small island in South Carolina.

THE SPARK

The afternoon of April 11, 1861, slaves rowed a small boat carrying three white men across the harbor from Charleston, South Carolina, to the island of Fort Sumter. The men were representatives of the Confederate States of America, bringing a message for the commander of the fort, U.S. Major Robert Anderson (1805–1871).

The message ordered Anderson to evacuate his troops immediately. Anderson politely refused. Fort Sumter belonged to the U.S. government, and he would not abandon it. However, Anderson did admit that his troops were almost out of food. If supplies were not delivered soon, the soldiers defending Fort Sumter might starve to death.

The path to this standoff began on December 20, 1860, when South Carolina seceded from the United States.

Anderson's command post had been located at Fort Moultrie on Sullivan's Island. But this fort's cannon was fixed on the open seas. When South Carolina seceded, it became the enemy behind Fort Moultrie's defenses.

So, under cover of darkness on December 27, 1860, Anderson and his troops relocated to the more defendable Fort Sumter. Whoever controlled Fort Sumter controlled access to Charleston, the South's most vital seaport.

Reaction to the movement of troops was swift. South Carolina troops occupied Fort Moultrie and Castle Pinckney, the other military installations in Charleston's harbor. Militia poured into the city and artillery was positioned on the Charleston Peninsula and surrounding islands. All guns sighted on Fort Sumter, where Anderson and his men were stationed.

PRIMARY SOURCES

Primary sources come from people who were eyewitnesses to events. They might write about the event, take pictures, post short messages to social media or blogs, or record the event for radio or video. The photographs in this book are primary sources, taken at the time of the event. Paintings of events are usually not primary sources since they were often painted long after the event took place. What other primary sources can you find? Why are primary sources important? Do you learn differently from primary sources than from secondary sources, which come from people who did not directly experience the event?

PS

STUDENT VS TEACHER

Major Robert Anderson was from Kentucky. Although a Southerner by birth, he was a steadfast supporter of the Union. Once an artillery instructor at West Point Military Academy, Anderson knew the power of the artillery aimed at Fort Sumter. He also knew the man commanding those guns. Brigadier General Pierre G.T. Beauregard (1818–1893) had been one of Major Anderson's prized artillery students at West Point. This was the nature of the Civil War. It pitted friend against friend and student against teacher.

A new president, Abraham Lincoln (1809–1865), had been elected in November 1860, but he would not take office until March. Meanwhile, the lame duck president, James Buchanan, meekly protested that South Carolina's secession was illegal, but he took no action to stop it. As the soldiers in Fort Sumter slowly ran low on supplies, more Southern states seceded.

Mississippi, Florida, Alabama, Georgia, Louisiana, and Texas all followed South Carolina out of the country. On February 4, 1861, these seven states formed a new nation—the Confederate States of America.

Military commanders in these states surrendered government installations and either headed north or, if their sympathies were with the South, joined the new Confederate Army. Soon, only two Southern military installations remained in control of the federal government. One was Fort Sumter.

> What happened at Fort Sumter would determine whether the United States split apart or went to war.

When Abraham Lincoln took office on March 4, he immediately faced a tough choice about Fort Sumter. If he ordered Major Anderson to abandon the fort, he would be admitting the Confederacy was an independent country with the right to control its own territory. But if Lincoln used the Navy to resupply the fort by force, the South could claim the Union had struck the first blow and war would likely follow.

The president chose a middle road. On April 4, he ordered a small flotilla to sail to Fort Sumter. Meanwhile, he notified South Carolina's governor that these vessels would peacefully resupply the fort. The ball was back in the Confederacy's court.

Illustration of the attack on Fort Sumter that appeared in the April 27, 1861, issue of *Harper's Weekly*

In the predawn darkness of April 12, the Confederate envoys returned to Fort Sumter with a final ultimatum: Evacuate or face immediate bombardment. Major Anderson still refused to leave. He escorted the envoys back to their boat. "If we never meet in this world again," he said as he shook the men's hands, "God grant that we may meet in the next."

At 4:30 a.m., a single mortar shattered the night silence. The shell rocketed high into the sky, exploding in a brilliant pyrotechnic display right over Fort Sumter. Artillery batteries on the other islands opened up, surrounding Sumter in a ring of fire.

The Civil War had begun.

VOCAB LAB

There is a lot of new vocabulary in this book. Turn to the glossary in the back when you come to a word you don't understand. Practice your new vocabulary in the **VOCAB LAB** activities in each chapter.

FORT SUMTER

Fort Sumter was part of a network of island forts constructed in the 1820s to defend the strategic Charleston Harbor against foreign enemies. The bay was also protected by Castle Pinckney and Fort Moultrie. Fort Sumter had been designed to hold 135 guns and garrison 650 men. However, on the eve of the Civil War, the fortification was still unfinished. The enlisted men's barracks were not completely built, and only 15 of the 135 cannons had been mounted.

Why did both the Union and the Confederacy place so much value on possessing Fort Sumter? Study this map for answers.

operations at Charleston
Leventhal

AMERICAN BOYS

In 1861, Elisha Hunt Rhodes was a 19-year-old from Pawtuxet, Rhode Island, and Sam Watkins was a 21-year-old from Columbia, Tennessee. Both young men were patriots prepared to defend their country.

On May 10, 1861, Watkins and 3,200 fellow Tennessee men boarded a train and headed off to fight for the Confederacy. The train chugged along at about 30 miles an hour. As it drove through towns, citizens lined the tracks to cheer for their troops. Ladies waved handkerchiefs. Men shouted, "Hooray for the Confederacy!" Watkins said, "Everyone was wild, nay, frenzied with the excitement of victory."[1]

Elisha Hunt Rhodes was only a few weeks behind Watkins. On June 19, 1861, he boarded a steamer for Washington, DC. A huge crowd gathered at the wharf to see the men off. Rhodes said he "went on board . . . with mingled feelings of joy and sorrow."[2]

> For four long years, Watkins and Rhodes fought for their "country."

They were both born in the United States. But by 1861, these two men had very different views of what it meant to be an American.

Their individual experiences are lenses through which the Civil War can be understood. From enlistment, through training and battle, to the days of victory and defeat, this book will follow the paths trod by Yankee Elisha Hunt Rhodes and Rebel Samuel Watkins through the Civil War.

PAST TO PRESENT

The Civil War was fought more than 150 years ago, but this conflict still casts a shadow over the present. The war launched an economic and racial revolution that transformed the country. It was a war about freedom—what it meant and who deserved it. It is impossible to fully understand the United States today without grappling with the causes and consequences of the war between the states.

The Civil War: The Struggle that Divided America shines a historian's spotlight on the Civil War. There are moments of glory, heroism, and extraordinary leadership. But with the gallantry came barbaric slaughter, stunning miscalculation, and national grief.

As part of your experience, you will dissect public and government documents to develop arguments for why each side went to war. You'll use math and maps to engineer military fortifications and understand battlefield strategy. To understand the victims of war's violence, you'll analyze and create visual art, photographs, and poetry.

Get acquainted with Elisha Hunt Rhodes and Sam Watkins. Train with them, march with them, and read their correspondence in order to understand the hopes and trials of patriots on both sides of the American Civil War.

VOCAB LAB

Write down what you think each word means. What root words can you find that help you? What does the context of the word tell you?

abolitionist, Confederacy, flotilla, fortification, secede, strategic, troops, and **Union**.

Compare your definitions with those of your friends or classmates. Did you all come up with the same meanings? Turn to the text and glossary if you need help.

KEY QUESTIONS

- Why was this a war in which so many brothers, friends, and colleagues were pitted against each other?
- Have you ever visited a Civil War battle site? What was it like? What did you learn there?

RATION OF TRUTH

The Civil War saw 4 million enslaved people freed, an estimated 750,000 soldiers die, and one united nation survive.

To investigate more, consider that recent scholarship suggests the casualty rate of the Civil War has been underestimated by as much as 20 percent. Research this claim. How do scholars calculate the casualty rate of a conflict? What are the arguments of historians who claim the casualty rate for the Civil War was as high as 850,000? Why does it matter if the casualty rate is off?

THE STATISTICS OF SLAUGHTER

From 1861 to 1865, 3 million Americans fought in the Civil War and at least 620,000, probably more, of them died. This was 2 percent of the United States' population, the largest death toll of any American war. But the military lost soldiers to more causes than death.

The casualty rate is a number that refers to military personnel removed from service because of death, wounds, sickness, capture, or because they are missing in action or have deserted. The Civil War had the largest casualty rate of all American wars. Do the math to evaluate the human toll this conflict took on a generation of Americans.

- **With an adult's permission, use the Internet to research the casualty rate for the Union and the Confederacy in the Civil War.** How did the following factors influence the casualty rates of both sides in the conflict?

  - Death from disease

  - Death from injury

  - Wounds

  - Captured or missing

  - Race of soldier

  - What state a soldier came from

  - What battle a soldier fought in

- **How can you plot this data?** Can you graph or chart these statistics in a way that educates people about the human toll of the Civil War?

- **Compare the casualty rate of the Civil War to those of other American wars.** What factors made the Civil War so deadly compared to wars that were larger in scope, such as World War II?

Chapter 1

The Roots of Rebellion

I WONDER IF THIS WHOLE THING COULD'VE BEEN AVOIDED. WHAT WILL COME FROM THIS WAR?

Why did slavery spark such outrage on both sides of the debate for and against it?

For some, slavery was a brutal system of forced labor that should be made illegal. For others, slavery was an economic necessity. These opposing viewpoints couldn't find common ground even as the government tried to forge compromises to keep both the North and the South happy.

The Civil War was fought because some states relied on slavery for their economic wellbeing, while other states believed slavery was cruel and should be outlawed. This tension simmered for decades. As the nation expanded, so, too, did slavery, and abolitionists and slavery's supporters butted heads at all levels—in the streets, on the fields, and in Congress. How did this debate begin?

One hot August day in 1619, colonists stood on the docks of Jamestown, Virginia, as a British ship sailed into the Chesapeake Bay. Survival in Jamestown, the first permanent British colony in North America, had been touch and go ever since it was founded in 1607. While the *White Lion* dropped anchor, colonists waited eagerly for supplies from home.

The ship carried an unexpected cargo—20 captive African men. The captain of the *White Lion* traded the Africans to the governor of Jamestown. So began the American system of racial slavery that lasted 246 years.

A SLAVE NATION

During the course of the seventeenth century, 13 British colonies were established along the Atlantic seaboard. Although slavery was legal everywhere, the southern colonies came to depend on slaves more than their northern neighbors. An elite class of Southern planters owned huge estates where they grew tobacco and cotton for export. Slaves were vital to this plantation economy.

By the 1760s, white colonists considered themselves in danger of becoming as enslaved as their black servants. The British Parliament passed taxes on tea, paint, paper, and other common goods. Britain's efforts to control trade galled Americans, who resented having to support a government 3,000 miles away. Through protests and pamphlets, boycotts and bullets, the colonists resisted what they labeled British tyranny.

On July 4, 1776, colonial leaders approved the Declaration of Independence, severing the fraying knot with their mother country of England. The Revolutionary War followed. Seven years later, the United States emerged victorious and free. The first national government of the new nation, called the Articles of Confederation, was ineffective, so in 1787, the founders went back to the drawing board to draft a new constitution. Slavery and states' rights immediately proved to be thorny issues.

Learn more about the first slaves at this website.

 African Americans Jamestown

THE NOVEL THAT SPARKED A WAR

In 1852, Cincinnati, Ohio, writer Harriet Beecher Stowe wrote *Uncle Tom's Cabin*.

A bestseller, the anti-slavery novel touched the emotions of Northerners in a way no abolitionist lecture or pamphlet had done before. Southerners scorned the book as false propaganda. This literature widened the cultural gap between the North and South. You can read it here.

 Uncle Tom's Cabin Gutenberg

THE CONSTITUTION AND SLAVERY

Throughout the sweltering summer of 1787, delegates to the Constitutional Convention gathered in Philadelphia, Pennsylvania, to craft a constitution. By this time, five of the Northern states had passed laws to gradually emancipate their slaves. But Southern states arrived at the convention determined to keep their property. Without slaves, their economy would fail.

The debate over what to do about slavery was heated. The convention was on the verge of collapse.

> To preserve unity, anti-slavery delegates gave in, and slavery was embedded in American law.

The Constitution protected slave owners in three ways. Three-fifths of a state's slave population was counted when determining how many representatives each state had in the U.S. House of Representatives. Because more slaves lived in the South than the North, this Three-Fifths Compromise increased the South's power in the U.S. Congress. The Constitution also barred Congress from banning the importation of slaves until 1808 and included a fugitive slave clause. This section of the document declared that even if a slave escaped to a free state, he remained a piece of property and must be returned to his owner.

Some leaders predicted slavery would die out naturally, but they were wrong. Rather than dying, slavery flourished.

The Schomburg Center for Research in Black Culture has a map on its website titled "The Illegal Slave Trade to the United States, 1808–1860." Why did these destinations appeal to slave smugglers?

In Motion illegal slave trade map

RATION OF TRUTH

Slavery is not specifically mentioned in the Constitution. The founders deliberately avoiding using the word, believing it would tarnish the document.

THE CONSTITUTION AND STATES' RIGHTS

The Founding Fathers did not want to create a central government with too much power, so they built the new republic on the principle of federalism. The Constitution divides power between the federal government and the states. But dividing power did not eliminate conflict. A struggle between the federal government and the states in the early nineteenth century hinted at the terrible war on the horizon.

In 1828, Northern lawmakers pushed a tariff through Congress to protect goods made in Northern factories from cheap European imports. This move infuriated Southerners, who relied on low-cost foreign products. Some Southerners wanted to secede over this "Tariff of Abominations."

South Carolina lawmakers proposed a drastic solution. In 1832, they passed the Ordinance of Nullification. This law argued the federal government existed at the will of the states. Therefore, if a state believed a federal law violated the Constitution, that state could declare the law null and void.

President Andrew Jackson (1767–1845) was having none of this. He sent a proclamation to South Carolina objecting to the nullification law. He even prepared to send troops into the state to enforce the tariff, but the crisis was averted when Congress revised the law. The issue of states' rights had reared its ugly head—it would not be the last time.

THWARTED DECLINE

During the Revolutionary War era, slavery declined. Inspired by the idea that "all men are created equal," some owners freed their slaves. A collapse in the tobacco market also made owning slaves more expensive. But in 1793, Eli Whitney invented the cotton gin, reversing slavery's decline. This cotton-cleaning machine made growing cotton more profitable. Within a decade, the value of the U.S. cotton crop skyrocketed from $150,000 annually to $8 million. Demand for slaves in the South increased. The 1790 census listed 697,897 slaves in the United States. By 1810, there were 1.2 million.

For more information about the growth of slavery, visit this website.

PBS Growth
of slavery

Consider the interactive map of the Missouri Compromise on the Teaching American History website. Between 1820 and 1821 do free or slave states dominate the U.S. Congress? What evidence is there for your conclusion?

 Teaching American History Missouri compromise map

The Civil War had a long fuse. The issues of states' rights, the role of the federal government, and the economy sparked conflict decades before the war began. At the core of all these issues was slavery.

- - - - - - - -

COMPROMISE AND RESISTANCE

As the nation expanded westward, slavery did, too. Politicians worked to balance the power of Northern free states and Southern slave states.

The first compromise was on the side of freedom. In 1787, the Northwest Ordinance established a territorial government for the region north and west of the Ohio River. Today, this includes the states of the Midwest. Slavery was outlawed in these territories.

In 1820, Missouri was admitted to the Union as a slave state, and Congress passed the Missouri Compromise. All territory west of Missouri, below 36 degrees north latitude, was open to slavery, while territory north of that line would be free. This compromise staved off conflict for 25 years.

Many enslaved people seized their freedom any way they could, including running away. The Underground Railroad was an informal network of black and white people who helped fugitives escape to freedom in Northern states or Canada. The exact number of enslaved people who fled on the Underground Railroad is unknown, but historians estimate between 25,000 and 40,000.

Other slaves rebelled. There were at least 250 documented slave insurrections prior to the Civil War. A man named Nat Turner (1800–1831) launched one in 1831. Inspired by religious conviction, he led an army of 40 men in an assault on slaveholders. They killed 57 white people in Virginia before the insurrection was stopped. Turner was caught, hanged, and his corpse was skinned. Another 55 slaves were executed. The revolt sparked hysteria throughout the South. White mobs murdered more than 200 blacks unconnected to the rebellion.[1]

A woodcut newspaper illustration of Nat Turner's rebellion

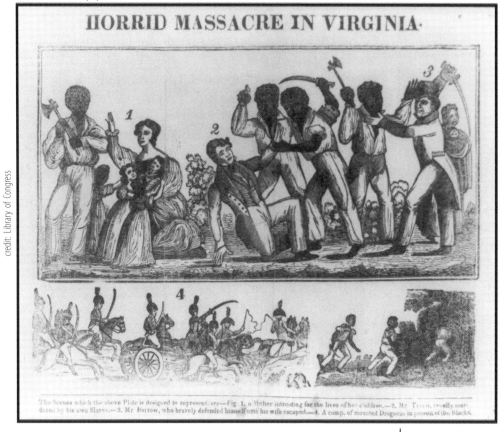

credit: Library of Congress

It was not only enslaved African Americans resisting slavery. In the 1830s, the abolitionist movement was born. This small but vocal group of reformers included white men and women as well as free blacks. They wrote pamphlets, editorials, and petitions demanding an immediate end to slavery. They organized anti-slavery societies and gave lectures in church halls and on street corners. Ridiculed and reviled, pelted with rotten eggs and sharp rocks, the abolitionists persevered. As America expanded westward and slavery ballooned, poor white farmers who feared competition from wealthy planters and their free slave labor joined the call to limit slavery.

WAR WITH MEXICO

From 1846 to 1848, the United States fought a war with Mexico over territory that belonged to Mexico but which the United States wanted. The United States won, gaining a swath of land in the Southwest that almost doubled the size of the nation. The ink on the peace treaty was barely dry before Americans took sides. Would the new Western territories be open to slavery or would they be free?

> The controversy rode roughshod through the halls of Congress and down main street America.

Slave owners believed if the Southwest was open to slavery, the institution would survive indefinitely. Northerners were convinced that if slavery was allowed to expand, the institution would eventually be legal everywhere. For two years, the debate pushed the United States closer to the brink of war. Then, in 1850, the Great Compromise yanked America back from the precipice. The reprieve was temporary.

A STACKED DECK

Before an alleged runaway was returned to the person claiming to be his owner, a hearing was held. However, neither the fugitive nor any other black person was allowed to testify. Commissioners who conducted the hearings were paid $10 for every slave returned to slavery, but only $5 for every person set free. The law had a built-in financial incentive for commissioners to turn a blind eye to injustice.

COMPROMISE WITH A CATCH

The Great Compromise threw a bone to both supporters and opponents of slavery. To please those against slavery, California was admitted into the Union as a free state, New Mexico and Utah were allowed to vote on whether they wanted slavery or not, and slave trading was banned in Washington, DC. For those who supported slavery, the Great Compromise included the tough, new Fugitive Slave Law. Rather than calming tensions, this law sparked outrage and activism.

The Fugitive Slave Law of 1850 required all citizens, whether they lived in a slave state or a free one, to help catch runaways. Slave catchers could travel into free states and claim a black person as a fugitive without having to show much proof. Free blacks were often kidnapped and sold in the South.

Even Northerners who did not support emancipation hated the Fugitive Slave Law. No state was truly free if slave hunters could roam at will. Law-abiding citizens became law breakers as the Underground Railroad grew. Northern states passed laws prohibiting state officials from aiding slave catchers. Free blacks established vigilante committees that rescued and sheltered runaways. By 1852, the number of captured fugitives dropped by two-thirds from the previous year.

The South grew angry. Southerners believed the federal government was unwilling to enforce the Fugitive Slave Law.

THE DRED SCOTT DECISION

A slave named Dred Scott (1799–1858) lived with his owner for several years in the free territories of Illinois and Wisconsin. In the 1840s, his owner returned to Missouri, Scott in tow. In 1846, Scott sued for his freedom on the grounds that living on free land had made him a free man. Scott lost, but appealed.

The case worked its way up to the U.S. Supreme Court. In 1857, the court struck a severe blow to enslaved people across the nation. In a 7-to-2 decision, the court said slaves were property, not people. Scott had no right to sue in court because African Americans, slave or free, were not citizens of the United States.

BLEEDING KANSAS

Because the territories of Kansas and Nebraska lay above the Missouri Compromise line, they should have become free states. But in 1853, Stephen Douglas (1847–1861), the Democratic senator from Illinois, introduced the Kansas-Nebraska Act that would permit citizens of these territories to vote on the slavery question. When the bill became law in 1854, Kansas exploded into a mini civil war that foretold the bloodshed to come. The New England Emigrant Aid Company of Massachusetts sent 1,200 armed men to Kansas to vote for freedom. Thousands of "Border Ruffians" flooded into Kansas from Missouri to turn Kansas into a slave state. Violence erupted, and 55 people died in this period called "Bleeding Kansas."[2]

In a final blow, the justices decreed that the Fifth Amendment to the Constitution prevented the government from depriving citizens of their property rights. This meant Congress could not limit the expansion of slavery in any Western lands. Political compromise over slavery was impossible.

JOHN BROWN'S RAID

If freedom would not come through the law, it must come from the sword. That was the philosophy of radical abolitionist John Brown (1800–1859). On October 16, 1859, the 59-year-old white man led five blacks and 13 whites into Harper's Ferry, Virginia. His goal was to seize the federal arsenal there, arm local slaves, and start a revolution. Just 36 hours later, most of Brown's men had been killed or captured.

RATION OF TRUTH

No slaves joined John Brown's rebellion on October 16, 1859.

John Brown's rebellion

credit: Library of Congress

Brown was severely wounded in the raid, captured, and turned over to the state of Virginia. He was quickly tried, convicted, and sentenced to be hanged. Before his December 2, 1859, execution, Brown passed his jailer a note: "I John Brown am now quite certain that the crimes of this guilty, land: will never be purged away; but with Blood."[3]

> Attitudes toward John Brown's rebellion revealed the ever-widening chasm between North and South.

Northerners hailed him as a martyr, while Southerners reviled Brown as a traitorous murderer. Distrusting the federal government's ability to protect them from violent abolitionists, Southerners called for secession.

A presidential election was scheduled for the fall of 1860. The man who won that contest would determine the future of the nation.

VOCAB LAB

Write down what you think each word means. What root words can you find to help you? What does the context of the word tell you?

boycott, **delegate**, **emancipate**, **federalism**, **injustice**, **insurrection**, **martyr**, **propaganda**, **tariff**, and **vigilante**.

Compare your definitions with those of your friends or classmates. Did you all come up with the same meanings? Turn to the text and glossary if you need help.

KEY QUESTIONS

- **How did the Underground Railroad contribute to tensions between free states and slave states?**
- **Why do some people point toward states' rights instead of slavery as the primary reason for the Civil War?**
- **Why did John Brown's raid spark such heated debate between the North and South?**

WANDERING THROUGH THE GAPS IN HISTORY

On November 28, 1858, the slave ship *Wanderer* slid up a coastal channel to the shores of Jekyll Island, Georgia, and secretly unloaded its slave cargo. The importation of Africans had been illegal since 1808. All ships were required to deliver a manifest to a customs agent at the port where they docked that listed all passengers on board. This document was required to prove blacks were legal slaves, not kidnapped victims from Africa. The *Wanderer*'s manifest is lost to history. Try to fill in the gaps.

- **Research and find examples of slave manifests online to determine what information the *Wanderer*'s manifest should include.**

- **Use the Transatlantic Slave Trade Database to fill in available historical information.** The *Wanderer* is listed in the "Voyages Database" for 1858.

  🔍 slave voyages

  - How successful were you at locating the required information?

  - What reasons might explain the fact that key information about the ship's cargo is missing?

- **Research to discover more about the *Wanderer*'s 1858 voyage.** Then redesign your manifest to tell a fuller story of the journey these Africans endured.

To investigate more, explore the impact of the *Wanderer* on the larger nation. How did news of this illegal importation of slaves affect the growing rift between the North and the South? How many other shipments of slaves were smuggled into the United States between 1808 and 1865 when the Civil War ended? What factors made it possible for this illegal trade to continue for so many years?

Chapter 2 ▶
Dueling Republics

WHY DO I SPEND SO MUCH TIME ON MY SPEECHES? WILL THEY EVER CARRY MUCH PURPOSE? HMM.....

How much of a factor was President Lincoln's victory in the start of the Civil War?

Many Southerners thought President Lincoln would take away their right to own slaves, while many Northerners thought the president would not do enough to end slavery—this tension added fuel to the already smoldering fire of conflict.

The 1860 election played a major role in the eruption of the Civil War. Had the nation elected someone who landed firmly on the side of the Southern states and openly supported slavery as an institution, history might have been very different. Instead, U.S. citizens elected Abraham Lincoln, a thoughtful president who believed the nation should not be divided.

Lincoln's views on slavery were another major spark that helped light the fuse of war. While he maintained that the South should be free to keep its slaves, he was against slavery on principle and did not want future states to allow slavery.

How might sSoutherners of the time view this new president? Why might they feel threatened?

A HOUSE DIVIDED

A raw wind blew across the campus of Knox College in Galesburg, Illinois, the afternoon of October 7, 1858. Political banners flapped and campaign signs flew. Spectators crowded around the platform erected against the wall of Old Main Hall.

A second-floor window opened and a short, round man stuck one stubby leg out the window and climbed down a ladder that was propped against the building. Seconds later, a gangly man emerged from the window, his legs unhinging like those of a grasshopper. The crowd drew closer, anxious to hear the debate between these two candidates running for U.S. Senate—Democrat Stephen Douglas (1813–1861) and Republican Abraham Lincoln.

A few months earlier, in June 1858, Abraham Lincoln had kicked off his bid for the Senate with a speech at the Illinois Republican convention. The Republican Party had just been founded in 1854.

> Opposition to slavery was a key point of the party's platform.

Lincoln's words at the Illinois Republican convention made history. Lincoln predicted, "A house divided against itself cannot stand. I believe this government cannot stand permanently half slave and half free."[1]

You can learn more about the Lincoln-Douglas debate at this website.

 NPS Lincoln Douglas

A stamp commemorating the Lincoln-Douglas debates

credit: U.S. Post Office

RATION OF TRUTH

Abraham Lincoln was not even on the ballot in the presidential election in 10 Southern states during the election of 1860.

Lincoln believed that stealing another man's labor was tyranny.

Now, he and Douglas faced off for their fifth debate. The issue on everyone's minds was the expansion of slavery in the West. Douglas believed the citizens of the states, not the federal government, should decide whether to allow slavery within their borders. Lincoln disagreed. While he opposed rooting out slavery in the Southern states, where it was already legal, he felt slavery was wrong and shouldn't be allowed to expand.

Douglas won reelection, but Lincoln won the larger battle for public opinion thanks to the new technology of the telegraph. Stenographers recorded every word in the debates in shorthand. They handed off their notes to runners, who hopped the next trains to Chicago. En route, these men transcribed the shorthand into text. From Chicago, the text of the debates were sent by telegraph to the rest of the country and were published in the newspapers.

Lincoln's status in the Republican Party skyrocketed. In 1860, Republicans set their sights on the White House with Abraham Lincoln as candidate for president.

THE BLACK REPUBLICAN

Slavery heated the nation to a boiling point during the presidential campaign of 1860. Southerners did not believe Lincoln's vow to leave slavery alone in the states where it was legal. The Democratic Party was weak because it was split over the issue of slavery. Northern Democrats nominated Lincoln's former opponent, Senator Stephen Douglas, but Southern Democrats did not think Douglas would fight hard enough to protect slavery in the West. They backed Senator John Breckinridge of Kentucky. To further muddy the political field, John Bell from Tennessee ran under the Constitution Party.

On November 6, 1860, Abraham Lincoln won the presidency. Three days after the election, the South Carolina legislature scheduled a convention to vote on whether or not to secede.

SESSION WINTER

On December 20, 1860, South Carolina voted to break off from the United States. The other cotton-growing states of the Deep South—Mississippi, Alabama, Georgia, Florida, Louisiana, and Texas—followed. In early February 1861, representatives from these states met in Montgomery, Alabama, and formed a new nation—the Confederate States of America.

These men drafted a constitution that was similar in many ways to the U.S. Constitution. The Confederacy had an executive branch with a president, a vice president, and a congress. One key difference was that slavery was explicitly protected in the law. Ironically, the Confederate Constitution did not allow a state to secede.

THE RAIL CANDIDATE

Born into a poor Kentucky family, Abraham Lincoln spent his youth splitting fence post rails and tilling fields. He had little formal schooling, but was rarely without a book in his pocket. As a young man, Lincoln moved to New Salem, Illinois. He worked as a clerk, joined the debating society, served in the Black Hawk War, became an attorney, and served four terms in the Illinois legislature. In 1846, Lincoln was elected to the U.S. House of Representatives, where he criticized the U.S. war with Mexico. In 1860, Lincoln ran for president as the "Rail Splitter," a man who would fight for working people.

Leaders in the U.S. Congress still held out hope for compromise and concessions. That winter, they worked to hash out a deal to bring the seceded states back into the Union. But the South refused to accept any agreement that did not permit slavery in the Western territories, and President Lincoln rejected any deal that did. The idea of compromise collapsed.

Meanwhile, the other slave states adopted a wait-and-see position. The states of the upper South—Arkansas, North Carolina, Tennessee, and Virginia—had strong economic ties to the Northern states of the Union. The border states of Delaware, Maryland, Kentucky, and Missouri knew that if they seceded, a powerful foreign power, the United States, would be their neighbor. All states waited for inauguration day.

RIVAL PRESIDENTS

In early February 1861, Jefferson Davis (1808–1889) was in the garden of his Mississippi plantation with his wife. A messenger arrived and handed him a telegram. Until January 21, Davis had been a U.S. senator. After Mississippi seceded, he bid farewell to his fellow senators, saying "This [secession] is done not in hostility . . . but from the high and solemn motive of . . . protecting the rights we inherited." Davis returned to Mississippi, hoping a crisis could be averted. Now, with dread, he read the telegram.

Davis's face paled and he winced as if in pain. The delegates at the convention in Montgomery had just elected him president of the Confederate States of America.

On February 18, Davis stood in front of Alabama's statehouse in Montgomery and took the oath of office. In his inaugural address, he discussed liberty, not slavery.

The inauguration of Jefferson Davis

credit: Archibald Crossland McIntyre

The inauguration of Abraham Lincoln

credit: Library of Congress

Davis recalled the principles of the Declaration of Independence, which granted the people the right to "alter or abolish" a government that had become "destructive." He insisted the Confederate states' actions were motivated "solely by the desire to preserve our own rights."

On March 4, it was Abraham Lincoln's turn. Much was riding on the tall man's words as he addressed the crowd. Desperate to convince the upper South and border states to remain in the Union, Lincoln urged Southerners to avoid haste as they considered their next steps. He put the burden of the country's future on the South's shoulders. "In your hands, my dissatisfied fellow countrymen . . . is the momentous issue of civil war." The North would not strike first. So, the Confederacy did.

RATION OF TRUTH

On Lincoln's inauguration day, the rooftops around the Capitol were lined with sharpshooters acting on rumors of a plot to assassinate the president.

A STUDY IN CONTRASTS

The difference in the leadership of Jefferson Davis and Abraham Lincoln is visible in their inaugural addresses. Davis waited until the day before his inauguration to write his speech. Lincoln sweated over his for six weeks. Davis's phrases were tortured, while Lincoln, in contrast, was poetic. You can read both speeches at these websites. What other comparisons can you make?

Lincoln inauguration speech

Jefferson Davis inauguration speech

ARMIES AND ALLIANCES

At 4 a.m. on April 12, the bombardment of Fort Sumter began. After a 36-hour artillery attack, Major Anderson raised a white flag above Fort Sumter. The first battle in the Civil War was a Confederate victory. It would not be its last.

Although Lincoln had promised not to strike the first blow, he had vowed to defend the nation. Now, he had to make good on that promise. In 1861, the U.S. Army had only 16,000 men, most of them stationed west of the Mississippi River. Many officers were Southerners by birth and now had to decide where their loyalties lay.

On April 15, President Lincoln called upon state militias to provide 75,000 volunteers to put down the South's rebellion. The Northern states responded quickly.

> So many men tried to enlist that some had to be turned away.

The South's response was fast as well—not good news for the Union. On April 17, Virginia voted to secede. The largest, richest slave state, which also bordered Washington, DC, was now the enemy.

Where Virginia went, so, too, went General Robert E. Lee (1807–1870). One of the most respected military commanders in 1861, Lee was asked by Lincoln to assume top command of the U.S. Army. Lee refused, insisting he could never draw his sword on Virginia. For the next two days, he paced in his garden and prayed on his knees and made a decision.

Lee resigned from the U.S. Army. Days later, Jefferson Davis made Lee a brigadier general in the Confederate Army. This was the first of many struggles Lincoln would endure as he tried to find the right man to lead his army.

Other states followed Virginia's lead. By the middle of May, North Carolina, Tennessee, and Arkansas had joined the Confederacy. Thousands of recruits flooded into Richmond, Virginia, the new Confederate capital.

Jefferson Davis kept one eye on Europe. The North had more people and more money. Davis needed an alliance with England, and he was convinced that England needed Southern cotton.

SLAVERY'S DEATH BEGINS

At the outset of the war, both Lincoln and Davis had clear goals. Davis insisted the Confederacy was a foreign country that wanted only to be left alone. He would fight a defensive war. Lincoln labeled the Confederates as rebels, refusing to recognize them as a foreign power. His goal was to reunite the nation, and he publicly promised federal troops would not interfere with "property." In other words, the Union Army would not liberate the slaves.

However, enslaved people did not wait to be liberated. The night of May 23, 1861, three men who had been digging embankments along the Chesapeake Bay for the Confederate Army stole a boat and rowed to Union-held Fort Monroe. According to the Fugitive Slave Law, these slaves had to be turned over to their owner. But General Benjamin Butler (1818–1893), the commander in charge of the fort, was a lawyer. He had other ideas.

RATION OF TRUTH

Of the 820 West Point graduates on active duty in April 1861, 184 resigned from the U.S. Army and enlisted in the Confederate Army.

The Civil War Trust website has a lot of information about the war, including articles on recruitment.

 Civil War Trust

Military law permitted a commander to seize enemy property being used for military purposes. When the slaves' owner came to collect the men, Butler refused. He called them "contraband of war."

President Lincoln allowed Butler's decision to stand. Word spread, and more slaves fled to Fort Monroe. Soon, 500 African Americans had sought sanctuary inside what they called "Freedom Fortress." These people were in a state of legal limbo, no longer slaves, but not yet free. However, by running toward freedom, enslaved people made Lincoln's pledge not to interfere with slavery useless. American slavery did not have long to live.

Both the North and South believed the war would be short—90 days, tops. Southerners hoped one decisive victory would convince the Union to let them go. Northerners believed one swift blow would convince the Confederacy it must stay. As the next chapter will demonstrate, the first battle of Bull Run in July 1861 revealed how tragically wrong everyone was.

VOCAB LAB

Write down what you think each word means. What root words can you find that help you? What does the context of the word tell you?

assassinate, **concession**, **convention**, **debate**, **hostility**, **inauguration**, **liberty**, **militia**, **principle**, and **telegraph**

Compare your definitions with those of your friends or classmates. Did you all come up with the same meanings? Turn to the text and glossary if you need help.

KEY QUESTIONS

- **What might have happened if Abraham Lincoln had not won the presidency?**

- **Lincoln claimed that he did not want to abolish slavery in states where it was already legal, but did not want to see it spread to other states as well. Do you think these are conflicting viewpoints? Why or why not?**

- **Is there any issue faced by the world today that is as divisive as slavery was in the 1800s?**

THIRD-PARTY POLITICS

The American political system is dominated by two political parties—the Democrats and the Republicans. Occasionally, a third party's involvement influences the outcome of an election. Investigate the impact third-party politics had on causing the Civil War.

- **Go to the website Voting America, 1840–2008 and examine the map titled "Presidential Election Voting."** Scroll across the animated timeline to reach "1860."

  voting America 1840

- **How did the introduction of a third-party candidate affect the outcome of this election?**

  - Which candidate would have benefited most if no third-party candidate had run in 1860? Why?

  - Would American democracy be stronger or weaker if more political parties had the influence and financing to field candidates as the Democrat and Republican parties do?

To investigate more, consider what other presidential election results have been significantly impacted by the involvement of a third party. If you were to create a new political party, what core issue would you campaign for? What would you name your party?

STATES' RIGHTS OR SLAVERY?

The Pew Research Center conducted a poll on the 150th anniversary of the start of the Civil War to explore Americans' beliefs about this conflict. The results indicated that 48 percent of Americans believe the Southern states seceded because of states' rights, and 38 percent of people believe the South seceded because of slavery. What does the historical evidence show? Gather a group of friends or classmates to do some research.

- **Go to this link to find the Declaration of Causes of the 13 Confederate States of America.**

 Civil War ordinances secession

- **Divide up the declarations so at least one person reads each state's justification for seceding.** As you read, list the reasons the state gives for leaving the Union.

- **As a group, categorize the reasons for secession.** Possible categories include slavery, states' rights, and economic concerns.

- **Visually portray how much each category influenced the South to secede.** Consider a pie graph, a word cloud, or an artistic representation.

- **Write a thesis on your visual representation, It should clearly state your group's conclusion about why the Confederate states seceded from the United States.**

> **To investigate more,** conduct your own informal poll to determine what views people have about the cause of the Civil War. Does their understanding conflict with what you discovered through reading the Declaration of Causes? If so, why do you think people do not have a clear understanding of what caused the Civil War?

Chapter 3 ▶
First Blood

What did the first battle of the Civil War show both the North and the South?

The number of dead, wounded, and missing people after the Battle of Bull Run was a sign that this war would not be as easily won as both sides thought. How might history have been different had the political leaders realized the length and deadliness of the war they were embarking on?

Northern and Southern men joined the ranks of their armies in droves, while leaders made plans to bring instant victory to their respective sides. But when the smoke cleared at Bull Run in Manassas, Virginia, everyone realized that the war could be longer and deadlier than they previously thought.

When Elisha Hunt Rhodes arrived in Washington with the 2nd Rhode Island Regiment in June 1861, he was both amazed and repelled. He wrote, "What a city! Mud, pigs, geese, Negroes, palaces, shanties everywhere."

Before the war began, Washington, DC, had a population of 75,000. After Lincoln's call for volunteers, thousands of soldiers flooded the city. Soldiers slept in the East Room of the White House and on its lawn. Troops billeted in the House and Senate chambers, crashed on committee room floors, and crammed into hallways. A sea of tents surrounded the city in a 3-mile radius.

On July 4, 1861, Lincoln asked Congress for 400,000 troops and $4 million. Brigadier General Irvin McDowell (1818–1885) took command of the army, and on July 16, he ordered troops to march west.

Elisha Hunt Rhodes was thrilled. The men filled their haversacks with three days' rations of salt pork and hardtack. Rhodes assumed they would march to Richmond, Virginia, and "give the Rebels a good pounding."[1]

A SHATTERED ILLUSION

Richmond was not the target. McDowell had his eyes on Manassas, Virginia, a small town 25 miles from Washington that served as a railroad junction. Confederate Brigadier General Pierre G.T. Beauregard and 22,000 Confederate troops protected this resource. Warned in advance that McDowell was on the way with 35,000 federal troops, Beauregard called for backup.

Steep banks lined the 40-foot-wide Bull Run River. McDowell arrived with his army of young soldiers. Most, including Elisha Hunt Rhodes, had never been tested in battle. McDowell delayed the attack while he planned his strategy.

Excitement about an anticipated Union victory was so high in Washington that some refused to stay home. Armed with picnic baskets and champagne, people drove carriages to the high ground overlooking Bull Run to cheer for the home team. What does this tell you about attitudes toward the war in the early days of the conflict?

SPY IN A HOOPSKIRT

The widow Rose Greenhow (1813–1864) was a well-known Washington, DC, socialite. Originally from Maryland, she was fanatically pro-Southern. Before the war began, Confederate leaders recruited her to lead a spy network in the heart of Washington. An attractive woman, Greenhow used her charms to wheedle secrets from government men. When she learned that General McDowell was marching for Manassas, Greenhow activated her spy ring. Sixteen-year-old Bettie Duvall hid a coded message in her hair and drove a wagon 20 miles to General Beauregard's headquarters. This tipoff spelled doom for the Union.

DEAD MAN WALKING

The Confederacy was not wealthy enough to outfit its soldiers properly. The shoes Sam Watkins wore were mass-produced, thin-soled, and fell apart quickly. Many Rebels went barefoot. After one battle, Watkins spotted a dead Yankee wearing a fine pair of boots and he decided to take them. As Watkins began to yank one of the boots off, he glanced at the dead man's face. "The colonel had his eyes wide open," Watkins recalled, "and seemed to be looking at me. I dropped that foot quick." That was the last time Watkins ever tried to steal from the dead.

The battle began at dawn on Sunday, July 21. Federal troops headed toward Stone Bridge, where they intended to cross Bull Run and simultaneously attack the north end of General Beauregard's line.

At first, all went according to plan. The Confederate line fell back. Back in the capital, Lincoln's spirits soared when he received a telegram that victory was practically guaranteed. However, these reports were premature. As Confederate Brigadier General Barnard Bee (1824–1861) frantically tried to rally his men, Brigadier General Thomas Jackson (1824–1863) and his Virginia brigade formed a line just over the crest of a hill. Union troops preparing to charge could not see them there.

> General Bee pointed at Jackson and allegedly bellowed to his scattered troops, "There stands Jackson like a stone wall! Rally behind the Virginians!"

These words made history. From then on, Thomas Jackson was known as "Stonewall Jackson."

The Virginians burst over the hill and released a volley of fire at the Federals. Once, twice, three times, McDowell's men assaulted the line of Rebels, but each time they slammed into a force field of fire. Then, Jackson ordered his men to "Yell like furies!" This was the first record of what became the infamous "rebel yell." The shrieking howl chilled the spine of every Yankee. The Federals turned and ran.[2]

Elisha Hunt Rhodes's company was in the brigade ordered to the front line to guard the Union retreat. They were the last to leave the field, and a Rebel battery pounded Rhodes's company when it reached Bull Run.

A sketch of the Battle of Bull Run

credit: Library of Congress

The Yanks stampeded Stone Bridge, but Rhodes chose the river instead, because on the bridge, men were dying like flies. Holding his gun above his head, Rhodes jumped in. The water reached up to his waist, but he made it across and joined the rest of the members of the Union Army in a retreat for their lives.

Thunder boomed like cannon fire and lightening ripped apart the sky as Rhodes staggered back to Washington that night. Many times, he wanted to lie down and give up, but friends urged him on. "I suffered untold horrors from thirst and fatigue," he later wrote. At dawn, Rhodes saw the spires of the capital city. He reached camp and collapsed inside his tent.

Read how the nineteenth-century magazine *Harper's Weekly* covered the first Battle of Bull Run and view artists' sketches of the battle. What special skills and characteristics would war correspondents and artists need to do their job well?

 Harper's Weekly 1861

WHAT'S FOR DINNER, BILLY YANK?

Menu

12 ounces of meat

Hardtack (a cracker also known as "teeth dullers")

Beans or peas

Rice

Coffee

Sugar

Vinegar

Salt and pepper

Potatoes

Molasses

Nightly Special: Skillygalee
Soak hardtack in cold water. Brown in pork grease and season to taste.

Review of Union Army Cuisine

"It was no uncommon occurrence for a man to find the surface of his pot of coffee swimming with weevils after breaking up hardtack in it; . . . but they were easily skimmed off and left no distinctive flavor behind."

The train carrying Confederate soldier Sam Watkins did not reach Manassas until the morning after the battle. Watkins was crushed. He feared the war had ended before he had even gotten a glimpse of a Yank. "Ah, how we envied those that were wounded," Watkins later wrote.

The consequences of the first Battle of Bull Run were profound. Although the casualty rate paled compared to future battles, 2,896 Union soldiers were killed, wounded, or missing. The Confederates' casualty rate was 1,982. Bull Run revealed how deadly this war would be.

> Many in the South crowed with pride, convinced the war was virtually over.

The defeat jolted the Union. Northerners had been arrogantly confident of a quick victory. Lincoln, afraid the Rebels might attack Washington, called an emergency cabinet meeting. The secretary of war put Baltimore, Maryland, on alert and ordered all militia regiments to defend the capital.

Lincoln ordered Washington fortified. Eventually, a 37-mile defense surrounded the city, including 68 forts, 20 miles of trenches, 800 cannon, and an army that ranged between 15,000 and 50,000 soldiers.

The House of Representatives passed a resolution to devote "every resource . . . for the suppression, overthrow, and punishment of rebels," and Congress authorized the recruitment of another 500,000 volunteers. Lincoln disbanded the Army of Northeastern Virginia that McDowell had led. He created a new fighting force called the Army of the Potomac and gave top command to a flamboyant, confident Major General George McClellan (1826–1885). It was a decision Lincoln would come to regret.

A photograph of Major General George McClellan by Matthew Brady, a famous Civil War photographer

credit: Library of Congress

RATION OF TRUTH

Different goals shaped different strategies. To unify the nation, federal troops must invade the South and force the Rebels to surrender. In contrast, the South wanted independence. For most of the war, the Confederate Army played defense on its own soil.

UNION STRATEGY

Nothing in Lincoln's life had prepared him to lead a nation during wartime. Therefore, he did what he had done all his life—he read books and sought advice. Ultimately, the Union developed a four-prong plan for victory.

First, the Confederacy must be invaded and its armies defeated. Lincoln asked Major General George McClellan to come up with a victory plan. On August 2, 1861, McClellan delivered an ambitious proposal known as the "Grand Strategy." Coordinated assaults against key targets would strike like a hammer to break the Confederacy's back.

Go to this PBS site to view a map of General McClellan's Grand Strategy. What is the key to its success? What is the best Confederate defense against the Union plan?

 PBS union grand strategy map

General Winfield Scott's Anaconda Plan

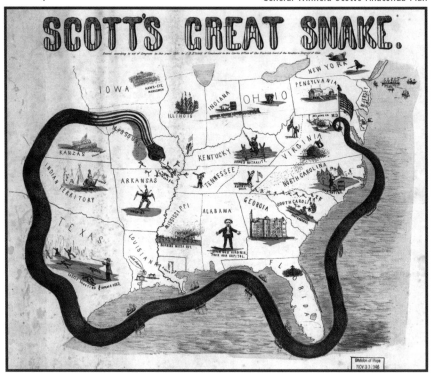

credit: Library of Congress

Former slave and editor Frederick Douglass claimed to know the quickest way to a Union victory. Read his article in *The Douglass Monthly* of May 1861. What war strategy does Douglass demand?

Douglass Monthly May 1861

Second, the Union would suffocate the South's economy. General Winfield Scott (1786–1866) developed the Anaconda Plan, a scheme to blockade all Southern ports. Union ships monitored the Confederacy's coastline, while federal gunboats patrolled the Mississippi River. Southern states could not supply each other or trade with Europe. However, the Northern navy had only 41 ships to monitor 5,000 miles of shoreline. This was not a quick solution.

The third element of the North's victory plan was to prevent Great Britain or France from aiding the Confederacy. By 1862, Lincoln realized that if he framed the war as a fight to abolish slavery, these anti-slavery nations would be reluctant to help the South. However, Lincoln feared any talk of ending slavery would alienate the border states.

Keeping the loyalty of Delaware, Kentucky, Maryland, and Missouri was vital for a Union victory. Washington was surrounded by Maryland on three sides. The Ohio River, a major waterway, ran through Kentucky, and one of the North's largest arsenals was located in St. Louis, Missouri. Although only 11 percent of the nation's slaves lived in the border states, public opinion over slavery was sharply divided in these regions. The president spent the first two years of the war walking a political tightrope as he tried to convince the people of the border states not to secede.

CONFEDERATE STRATEGY

The goal of the Confederacy was independence. Therefore, Rebel armies did not need to invade the North, only defend the South. But self-defense required manpower, and the South had fewer people than the North. With that in mind, General Lee aimed to strike hard at federal troops, even when outnumbered. He aimed to break the morale of northern citizens.

> If the people tired of war, they would demand President Lincoln negotiate peace.

Cotton also figured in the Confederate war strategy. This Southern crop fueled the textile mills of Europe, and President Davis was counting on Great Britain's desire to protect its cotton market. Even before the Battle of Fort Sumter, Davis sent a team of diplomats to England to negotiate an alliance. However, Great Britain had stockpiled surplus cotton in 1861 and was in no hurry to enter the war. The rest of Europe, too, just sat back and waited for the Rebels to prove they were worth backing.

CONSTITUTIONAL OVERREACH

Following the Battle of Fort Sumter, Maryland scheduled a convention to vote on secession. On the eve of the election, Lincoln ordered the arrest of Baltimore's mayor and 31 state legislators because of their pro-Confederate views. According to the Constitution, if a person believes he has been wrongly detained, he can ask the court for a writ of habeas corpus. This document requires law enforcement to bring the accused before a judge and to explain why the person is being held. However, Lincoln suspended this protection. The Maryland men spent months in jail until a pro-Union state legislature was elected in November of 1861.

LITTLE MAC STANDS STILL

Impressed by the Grand Strategy of Major General George McClellan, Lincoln appointed him commander of the Army of the Potomac and, in November 1861, general-in-chief of all Union armies. McClellan was only 34 years old.

McClellan's first priority was to whip the army of green recruits into fighting form. For six months, the army remained in Washington and trained. Elisha Hunt Rhodes grew sick of drilling in the "mud, mud, mud," but, like the rest of the soldiers, he loved "Little Mac," as General McClellan was fondly called.

President Lincoln, however, grew frustrated as month after month, McClellan refused to engage the enemy. McClellan was convinced a massive Rebel force awaited him in Virginia. At the time, the Union Army numbered 120,000, and across the Potomac River the Confederates had only 45,000 men. But McClellan refused to believe these numbers.

Meanwhile, in the West, Union General Ulysses S. Grant was on the move.

WHAT'S FOR DINNER, JOHNNY REB?

Menu

Bacon (substitution lard or mule)

Cornmeal (unsifted and gritty)

Wheat flour (reserved for sick soldiers)

Coffee (None available. Try homemade brew of parched peanuts, peas, dried apples, or corn.)

Nightly Special: Coosh
Fry bacon until pan is half-full of grease. Mix cornmeal with water and then pour into hot grease, stirring until brown gravy forms. Add onion. Roll dough in a coil, wrap around bayonet, and cook over the fire.

Review of Confederate Army Cuisine

"A buzzard wouldn't eat this meat."

KEY QUESTIONS

- Why is the first battle in a war a very important one?
- What is the connection between the way a soldier is treated and how well he performs in war? Do you think soldiers who are hungry and tired can fight well?
- Do you think Lincoln made a mistake in appointing an overly confident man to a major leadership position?

PREDICTING VICTORY

When the Civil War began, which side had the advantage in terms of resources? Predict the victor based on the numbers.

- **Develop a list of resources needed for military victory.** Consider population, value of manufactured goods, miles of railroad tracks, coal production, and the value of agricultural production.

- **Create a data graph to compare the resources of the Union and the Confederacy in 1861.** Which type of graph presents the clearest comparison: bar graph, line graph, pictograph, or pie graph?

- **Based on this information your data reveals, make a prediction.** Who was best positioned to win in 1861?

To investigate more, ask what change in resources could have altered the outcome of the war? Why? What factors might have influenced this resource, such as disease, weather, or new innovations? Reconsider your predictions to allow for potential changes in different resources.

FIGHTING MUSIC

When soldiers marched to war, they took along their love of music. Songs helped fire the spirit and forge unity. The song "The Battle Cry of Freedom" was composed by George Root in 1862. The song was very popular, and so William H. Barnes penned Confederate lyrics that were sung by Rebels. Analyze both Union and Confederate versions of this song to figure out why this music was so inspirational. Then write your own lyrics.

* **Go to this website to find a recorded excerpt of an instrumental version of "The Battle Cry of Freedom"** and side-by-side lyrics of the Union and Confederate versions of the song.

    Civil War
    Heritage lyrics

    * How are these lyrics similar and how do they differ?

    * How does each version symbolize the cause for which the soldiers were fighting?

* **Write new lyrics for a modern, unified United States.** What patriotic ideals are in your modern version that were also present in both nineteenth-century versions?

> **To investigate more,** compare music from the Civil War to the most popular songs of World War I and World War II. How does war music change through time and how does it remain constant?

Chapter 4

Back-and-Forth Butchery

THE DEAD ARE HEROES, THE LIVING ARE BUT MEN COMPELLED TO DO THE DRUDGERY AND SUFFER THE PRIVATIONS INCIDENT TO THE THING CALLED "GLORIOUS WAR."

How did the first battles of the Civil War foretell what the war was going to be like?

GENERAL GRANT AT THE FIRST UNION VICTORY IN 1862

NO TERMS EXCEPT AN UNCONDITIONAL AND IMMEDIATE SURRENDER....

GENERAL MCCLELLAN WAS TRICKED

SIR! NO REBELS, BUT PLENTY OF EMPTY OYSTER SHELLS AND HALF-BAKED BISCUITS.

GENERAL LEE TOOK OVER THE ARMY OF NORTHERN VIRGINIA.

HE LOOKS TO ME LIKE SOME GOOD BOY'S GRANDPA.

The first battles were horror scenes of brutal carnage in which even the victors seemed like losers since they lost so many soldiers. This pattern would become evident again and again during the long years of war ahead.

The first few battles of the Civil War set the stage for the long, bloody trial that would follow for both sides. Even as soldiers were slaughtered on the fields of battle, each government maintained that it was in the right and the stand it was taking was justified. While government and military leaders struggled to find ways of gaining ground and maintaining morale, soldiers and witnesses were traumatized by the pure carnage they encountered. The first of these scenes took place in Tennessee in early February.

Icy winds whipped snow and sleet into the faces of Union soldiers huddled under leaves in the woods near Fort Donelson, Tennessee, on February 13, 1862. The day before, the sun had blazed as the army of Union General Ulysses S. Grant (1822–1885) marched cross-country toward the heavily guarded Confederate garrison that controlled access to the Cumberland River. Federal troops, convinced spring was here to stay, tossed aside blankets and overcoats.

Then, the sun went down, and so did the temperature. Grant did not want the Rebels to spot Union positions, so he banned all fires. As dawn broke on Valentine's Day, there was little love for their enemy in the frozen Yankees' hearts.

UNCONDITIONAL SURRENDER

The Cumberland River loops through Tennessee into the Ohio River. To secure Tennessee, Confederates constructed Fort Henry on the Tennessee River and Fort Donelson just below the Kentucky border, along the Cumberland River. On February 6, 1862, Grant easily seized the small, poorly defended Fort Henry, and then set his sights on Fort Donelson. A much more formidable target, the fort was defended by 20,000 Rebels, 5,000 more men than Grant commanded.

Grant ordered Rear Admiral Andrew Hull Foote to use his flotilla of ironclad and wooden gunboats to attack Donelson's batteries from the river. This strategy had worked at Fort Henry. But Fort Donelson was not Fort Henry. Within range of Confederate batteries, the flotilla endured a cruel barrage of fire. The Union commander of one boat said, "There was so much blood on [the decks] that our men could not work the guns without slipping."[1]

As another frigid night fell, Union soldiers listened to the Rebels celebrate inside the fort. It was a tough sound to hear. But what they didn't know was that inside the fort, four Confederate generals squabbled about their next move.

At 6 in the morning, a rebel yell shattered the icy air. The Confederate attack was ferocious and effective. Union troops ran out of ammunition and one line after another crumpled. By the afternoon, Rebels had carved a way out of the fort.

THE HORSEMAN

Historian Shelby Foote wrote that General Grant had "four o'clock in the morning courage." If wakened from a solid sleep with disastrous news, he calmly assessed the situation and acted. Elisha Hunt Rhodes saw Grant when the general came to review his army on April 18, 1864. Rhodes wrote, "General Grant [was] a short thick set man and rode his horse like a bag of meal. I was a little disappointed in the appearance, but I like the look of his eye."

General Grant and a horse

credit: Library of Congress

Then, disagreement between the four generals rose up again and, in the distraction, victory was snatched from the South's grasp. Soon, the troops retreated back inside the fort. Grant rode along the front line as the Union lines rallied and moved forward to block any Confederate advance. When the sun rose on February 16, a Confederate delegate under a white flag requested a meeting to discuss surrender terms.

> Grant's reply was curt and clear. "No terms except an unconditional and immediate surrender . . . ."

The Union Army took 12,000 prisoners and tens of thousands of arms, artillery, and horses. Seizure of Fort Donelson guaranteed that Kentucky would remain firmly in Union hands. Lincoln promoted Grant to major general, and the media nicknamed him "Unconditional Surrender Grant." He was the man of the hour.[2]

THE PENINSULAR CAMPAIGN

At midnight on March 10, 1862, the Army of the Potomac in Washington, DC, finally received word that it was heading to war. Still convinced a massive Confederate force waited across the Potomac River, General McClellan had decided to avoid this army by floating 100,000 soldiers down the Chesapeake Bay to land at Fort Monroe. Then, they would march up the Virginia peninsula and attack Richmond from the southeast. As part of the Grand Strategy, other generals would strike Rebel forces in the Shenandoah Valley and the Allegheny Mountains.

ELIZABETH KECKLEY

Former slave and skilled seamstress Elizabeth Keckley (1818–1907) was dressmaker to First Lady Mary Todd Lincoln. In the summer of 1862, Keckley witnessed the flood of escaped slaves pouring into the capital. These refugees lived in overcrowded, filthy housing. When Keckley saw wealthy white people give garden parties to raise funds for wounded soldiers, she was inspired. Keckley founded the Contraband Relief Society, which raised funds and distributed clothing to runaways.

You can read Keckley's autobiography at this website. At the time it was published in 1868, it was considered fairly controversial because of the information it revealed about the Lincolns.

Keckley autobiography

On March 17, 400 vessels carrying men, horses, tents, artillery, ambulances, telegraph equipment, and supplies launched into the Chesapeake Bay. They disembarked at Fort Monroe and began to plod up the Virginia peninsula. Hampered by poor maps, high rivers, and lots of mud, the army reached Yorktown on April 5. There, McClellan halted again.

Yorktown was defended by General John Magruder and 11,000 Rebel soldiers. This force was dwarfed by McClellan's army. But Magruder played an old trick on his Yankee opponent. He ordered troops to march past the clearing in the woods so they could be seen from the Union lines. Then, these same soldiers doubled back and marched past again. They did this over and over, all day long. Magruder ordered his artillery wheeled to and fro, firing heavily when federal soldiers were spotted. To Union scouts, the Confederate army appeared massive.

McClellan was fooled. He sent a telegraph to Washington notifying Lincoln that he would not attack Yorktown, but lay siege to it instead.

Lincoln was livid. "You must act!" he ordered. McClellan ignored him.

The siege of Yorktown dragged on. Rain fell daily and Union soldiers sickened. Meanwhile, the largest Confederate Army, known as the Army of Northern Virginia, moved onto the peninsula with General Joseph Johnston (1807–1891) in charge.

The morning of May 4, McClellan finally ordered an assault on Yorktown. Troops entered the city to discover the Confederate camp deserted. Johnston had evacuated the night before. All that remained of the massive Rebel army were oyster shells and half-baked biscuits.

McClellan pursued Johnston's army to just outside Richmond. But then, he stopped again, refusing to attack until Lincoln sent 40,000 reinforcements. Secretary of War Edwin Stanton was irate. He said, "If he had a million men, he would swear the enemy had 2 millions, and then he would sit down in the mud and yell for three." Lincoln did not send reinforcements.[3]

At the end of May, General Johnston attacked the Union forces on the south side of the Chickahominy River. The action achieved nothing and Johnston was badly wounded. President Davis turned over command of the Army of Northern Virginia to General Robert E. Lee, a bold leader who had the uncanny ability to predict the moves of his opponents. One day, Sam Watkins spotted Lee in camp. The general, who sported Santa Claus-style whiskers, reminded Watkins of some "good boy's grandpa," in part because the general had eyes as "as gentle as a dove."

Lee's eyes may have been gentle, but his strategy was not. Outnumbered almost two to one, Lee went on the offensive. Like a dog with a bone, he would not let up. From June 25 to July 1, the two armies fought six battles within seven days. The relentless fighting hammered the Union Army. Supplies ran low. Men slept outside in constant rain. "May God help us," Rhodes wrote in his diary.

The Rebels shoved Union troops back down the peninsula to Yorktown over the same muddy ground they had trudged only weeks earlier. Disappointed by McClellan's paralysis, Lincoln sent him to guard Washington and put General John Pope in charge of the army. This change did not help. On August 30, the Rebels scored another victory in the Second Battle of Bull Run.

THE MARBLE MAN

Robert E. Lee had deep American roots. His father fought in the American Revolution, two uncles signed the Declaration of Independence, and Lee's wife was George Washington's great-granddaughter. Lee graduated second in his class at West Point and distinguished himself in the Mexican War. Although Lee disapproved of secession, he also condemned the North's attitude toward the South. When Virginia seceded, Lee followed his state out of the Union because, he believed, "I could have taken no other course without dishonor."

General Robert E. Lee

credit: Library of Congress

RATION OF TRUTH

General McClellan showed disdain for President Lincoln in public and private. In a letter to his wife, McClellan referred to the president as "nothing more than a well meaning baboon." Lincoln tolerated the disrespect as long as he believed the general could lead the North to victory, saying once that he would "cheerfully stand and hold McClellan's horse for him if only he would give us a victory."

Lincoln reinstated McClellan as top commander. He knew the general had flaws, but Union troops were so demoralized, he believed only McClellan could lead them. While the Union Army retreated in the East, the war reached a stalemate in the West and the death toll kept climbing.

BLOODBATH IN THE WEST

On Sunday April 6, 1862, the meadow surrounding the little church of Shiloh on the banks of the Tennessee River turned from green to red. Confederate forces surprised the army of General Grant, and in two days, the nation saw carnage on a scale never before witnessed.

Watch the animated summary of the Battle of Shiloh at this link. What factors helped the Union force the Confederates to retreat?

 Shiloh animated

RATION OF TRUTH

The casualty rate of *all* previous American wars combined to that point was close to 35,000.

The battle began when Union soldiers were preparing breakfast. At noon, Sam Watkins and Company H were ordered to advance to the front lines. Watkins walked in a dream-like state over a field strewn with dead and dying horses and men. Suddenly, "Siz, siz, siz, the minnie balls from the Yankee line began to whistle" past his head. Watkins had been feeling "mean all morning." When the order came to fix bayonets and charge, Watkins was elated.

> "I shouted. It was fun then.
> Everybody looked happy."

Watkins did not stay happy. Union reinforcements arrived, and the following day, the Rebels retreated. In only two days at Shiloh, there were more than 23,741 casualties. But the bloodshed at Shiloh was soon to be outdone.

THE BLOODIEST DAY

By early September of 1862, 50,000 Confederate troops were camped about 40 miles from Washington. Although General McClellan commanded 85,000 federal soldiers, Lee decided to strike the Union hard on Northern soil.

On the morning of September 13, a Union corporal spotted a bulky envelope on the ground. Inside were three cigars wrapped in a document. Confederates had recently camped in this spot, and the document was a copy of Special Order No. 191—Lee's plan to divide his army and attack McClellan's forces. General McClellan telegraphed President Lincoln. "I have all the Rebel plans and will catch them in their own trap."

The Battle of Shiloh by Thure de Thulstrup

credit: Library of Congress

But McClellan did not spring the trap. Cautious as always, he waited four days before advancing on Lee's center. By that time, six of Lee's nine divisions had reunited along Antietam Creek near Sharpsburg, Maryland. A climactic battle was about to begin.

At dawn, 1,000 Union soldiers crawled through a cornfield toward Confederate lines. The corn stood tall and shielded their approach. But 200 yards away, Georgia soldiers lay on their bellies, waiting. When the Yankees burst from the cornfield, the Confederates fired. That cornfield exchanged hands 15 times that day. Major General Joe Hooker later reported that, "Every stalk of corn in the great part of the field was cut as closely as could have been done with a knife."

By noon, Federals shifted their attack to the Sunken Road, an old path that ran 5 feet below ground level. Rebels hunkered inside Sunken Road, about 2,000 of them. Colonel John B. Gordon vowed his men would defend the lane until victory or sunset.

Despite heavy Rebel fire, Union forces encircled the road and turned it into a death trap. Gordon was hit twice in the leg, once in the arm, again in the shoulder, and finally in the face. The bodies of Confederate soldiers lay three deep. Sunken Road was renamed "Bloody Lane."

Union General Ambrose Burnside fought for hours to move his 12,500 men over a bridge under a bluff held by Confederates. Burnside ordered four charges over that bridge, but his men were repelled every time. The Federals finally crossed the bridge on the fifth charge.

> They stormed the bluff, only to be pushed back across the bridge when Rebel reinforcements arrived.

On the day the battle of Antietam broke, Elisha Hunt Rhodes was in the nearby hills chasing Confederate cavalry. He stood on a cliff and watched the action play out below. Waves of blue and gray clashed, the cries of the men and roar of artillery reaching Rhodes's ears a split second later. "I have never in my soldier life seen such a sight," Rhodes wrote that night. "The dead and wounded covered the ground."

The battle raged for 12 hours. September 17, 1862, remains the bloodiest single day in American history—23,000 men were dead, wounded, or missing. Neither side gained any ground.

THE PICTURE OF DEATH

The Civil War was the first American conflict documented in photographs. As a young man, Mathew Brady (1823–1896) learned daguerreotype, an early photographic process that stamped an image on a metal plate. He opened his own studio in New York City in 1844. When the war began, Brady hired a crew of photographers to record the conflict, including Alexander Gardner (1821–1882). Two days after the Battle of Antietam, Gardner photographed the dead on the battlefield. These images were displayed at Brady's gallery.

Lincoln and McClellan meet

credit: Alexander Gardner, Library of Congress

The next morning, the Rebels retreated back across the Potomac. McClellan had the manpower to pursue them, and Lee braced for an attack. President Lincoln telegraphed McClellan, urging him to "Destroy the Rebel army if possible." McClellan did not move.

Lincoln's patience was just about up. He visited the Union Army encampment in Maryland to meet with McClellan. First, he urged the general to pursue Lee's army. Then he ordered him. Still, McClellan resisted, insisting he needed more men.

You can find photographs of the Battle of Antietam at the National Park Service site. What do these photographs reveal about the Civil War?

Warning: These images could be disturbing for some viewers.

 NPS Antietam historic photographs

VOCAB LAB

Write down what you think each word means. What root words can you find that help you? What does the context of the word tell you?

barrage, **carnage**, **daguerreotype**, **paralysis**, **refugee**, **reinforcement**, **stalemate**, and **surrender**.

Compare your definitions with those of your friends or classmates. Did you all come up with the same meanings? Turn to the text and glossary if you need help.

Lincoln had had enough. On November 5, 1862, the president removed McClellan from command. The general went home to await his next orders. They never came.

The Battle of Antietam had long-lasting consequences.

At Antietam, the Union Army stopped the Confederate invasion of the North. President Jefferson Davis desperately needed an alliance with Great Britain or France, but after the Rebels retreated from Antietam, both nations decided to sit out the war.

From a military perspective, the Battle of Antietam was a virtual tie. But Lincoln was able to cast it as a victory in order to make a bold political move to transform the war into a fight for freedom.

KEY QUESTIONS

- **Why was General McClellan so hesitant about attacking Confederate troops?**
- **How might the Battle of Antietam have been different if McClellan had attacked earlier? How might the war have gone differently?**
- **Why did foreign powers decide not to engage in the Civil War? What impact do you think this decision had on the outcome of the war?**

PICTURING POETRY

In 1866, Herman Melville (1819–1891) published a
book of war poems, including one titled "Shiloh: A
Requiem." A requiem is a composition meant to be
performed at a funeral.

Shiloh: A Requiem (April, 1862)

Skimming lightly, wheeling still,
    The swallows fly low
Over the field in clouded days,
    The forest-field of Shiloh–
Over the field where April rain
Solaced the parched ones stretched in pain
Through the pause of night
That followed the Sunday fight
    Around the church of Shiloh–
The church so lone, the log-built one,
That echoed to many a parting groan
    And natural prayer
    Of dying foemen mingled there–
Foemen at morn, but friends at eve–
    Fame or country least their care:
(What like a bullet can undeceive!)
    But now they lie low,
While over them the swallows skim,
    And all is hushed at Shiloh.

- **Read this poem out loud several times.** Sketch
  the images that come to mind as you listen to
  the text. Compare your sketch to that of a friend.
  How did your visual interpretations of this poem
  compare?

> **To investigate more,**
> read Chapter I of *What
> I Saw at Shiloh*, from
> a memoir written by
> Ambrose Bierce. Draw
> a sketch of what you
> imagine this scene to
> look like. Compare
> this sketch to the
> one you drew about
> Melville's poem. How
> are these two writers'
> interpretations of the
> Battle of Shiloh similar
> and different?

To investigate more, think about which Civil War battles might have been most affected by the telegraph. What other technologies played an important role in the Civil War?

HOW THE TELEGRAPH CHANGED THE WAR

A communication revolution began in 1844 with Samuel Morse's invention of the telegraph machine. By 1860, there were 50,000 miles of telegraph lines across the country. When a telegraph office opened up next door to the White House, it effectively became President Lincoln's situation room.

Messages sent by telegraph are in Morse code. Dots and dashes, written or transmitted by sound, correspond to letters in the alphabet. Investigate how telegraph technology works and build your own machine. Go to this link to try your skills at Morse code.

🔍 learn Morse code

- **Research the Internet for the basics on how a telegraph machine works.** Compare different blueprints for how to build your own simple telegraph machine.

- **Follow the directions of the model you choose.** Or, combine elements of two or more models to create your own design.

- **Try to make a sound with your machine.** If it does not work, what adjustments can you make to increase the power of the electromagnet?

- **Send a Morse code message on your machine.** Ask a friend to transcribe it. Can your friend decipher your message correctly? How can you modify your machine to communicate across longer distances?

Chapter 5
A New Birth of Freedom

YOU KNOW? THEY SAY THAT WE ARE FREE! WHY DO WE KEEP WORKING?

How did the Emancipation Proclamation affect the war?

When President Lincoln outlawed slavery in the Southern states, he was met with both cheers and jeers. Some people rallied to fight for the sake of freedom for all, while others felt unification was the more important issue. In the South, most people heartily rejected the Emancipation Proclamation.

One morning in June 1862, President Lincoln went to the War Department's telegraph office across the street from the White House. He often spent long hours there, communicating with commanders on the battlefield. On this day, Lincoln asked Major Thomas Eckert for paper. The president sat by the window and wrote, taking breaks occasionally to watch a spider spin a huge web outside the window.

Before he left, Lincoln gave his writing to Eckert for safekeeping. The words Lincoln wrote that day were revolutionary. They would enrage, inspire, and embolden.

Abraham Lincoln believed slavery was a "moral, social, and political evil."[1] The lawyer in him knew it was illegal to seize the property of Southerners, and slaves were considered property. However, as the war bogged down, the cries of abolitionists to emancipate the slaves grew louder.

Quakers visited Lincoln at the White House to tell him that, as God's instrument, he must immediately free all those in bondage. Former slave and editor Frederick Douglass (1818–1895) wrote a column and laid out a choice for the nation: "You must abolish slavery or abandon the union."

The president knew something had to change. His popularity hovered at 25 percent and midterm congressional elections would be held in November. Lincoln's change in strategy was to outlaw slavery in the Confederacy.

CHANGING TACTICS

The document Lincoln had drafted at the telegraph office was his new game plan. On September 22, a few days after the Battle of Antietam, the president announced the Preliminary Emancipation Proclamation. Confederate states had three months to lay down their weapons and rejoin the Union if they wanted to keep their slaves. On January 1, 1863, Lincoln would sign the Emancipation Proclamation into law, and all slaves in states still in rebellion would "thenceforward, and forever, be free."

Parades, bonfires, and rallies followed Lincoln's announcement. Abolitionists were thrilled that Lincoln had finally landed on the side of abolishing slavery.

However, not everyone was pleased. Around 4 million slaves lived in the United States, but the Emancipation Proclamation applied to only 3.1 million of them. Slavery would remain legal in the border states. Editor William Lloyd Garrison was disgusted. He described Lincoln as "6 feet 4 inches high, [but] he is only a dwarf in mind."[2]

Frederick Douglass

credit: Library of Congress

You can read Frederick Douglass's column at the Teaching American History website.

 Teaching History slaveholders rebellion

Democrats were upset, too, because the proclamation went too far. *The New York Herald* said emancipation would lead to racial insurrection and blacks would "massacre white men, women, and children till their hands are smeared and their appetites glutted with blood."

Reaction from the troops in the field was also mixed. Some soldiers were eager to fight for freedom. Elisha Hunt Rhodes recorded in his diary, "I thank God that I have had an opportunity of serving my country, freeing the slaves, and restoring the Union."

> Soldiers hoped Lincoln's move would shorten the war.

However, there was condemnation from the field as well. A New York soldier "wished all abolitionists were in hell." General McClellan even considered resigning, convinced the proclamation would lead to massive slave revolts.

Enslaved people did not wait for the proclamation to take effect. Instead, they began to walk north, looking for the enemy lines so they could leave behind their lives of slavery. Owners moved their slaves deep into Southern territory so they could not flee to Union lines. But even those who could not escape had a new attitude. One Alabama mistress complained her slaves refused to do any chores. "They say they are free."

Not a single Confederate state took Lincoln up on his offer. To make matters worse, on December 15, Union forces led by General Ambrose Burnside suffered a brutal defeat at the Battle of Fredericksburg, suffering more than 12,000 casualties. Northern morale shattered and desertion rates soared. President Lincoln sank into a deep depression.[3]

COLONIZATION

The American Colonization Society's solution to the "problem" of what to do with emancipated slaves was to resettle them in distant lands such as Panama, Haiti, and Liberia. However, most blacks had no desire to leave the United States. This was their home. President Lincoln favored colonization. "The emigration of colored men," he said, "leaves additional room for white men." Although some African Americans moved to West Africa and established the nation of Liberia, by 1863, colonization was abandoned as expensive, impractical, and unpopular.

A NEW DAY, A NEW YEAR

New Year's Day dawned cold and gray. At 11 in the morning, ushers opened the White House to visitors. Lincoln spent hours shaking hands with hundreds of well-wishers. Finally, at 2 in the afternoon, he slipped into his office. In the center of his desk lay a document. Lincoln dipped a pen in the inkwell, but then paused, his hand trembling from all those hours of greeting people. Lincoln picked up the pen again. "If my name ever goes into history," he told the staff gathered around, "it will be for this act, and my whole soul is in it."

There was an important change between the preliminary proclamation announced in September 1862 and the final version signed on January 1, 1863. In the initial proclamation, Lincoln declared slaves in the Confederacy "are . . . *forever* free." However, Lincoln knew only a constitutional amendment could abolish slavery permanently. So he changed the document to read slaves "*shall be* free." The change signified hope, but was no guarantee of permanent freedom.

A soldier reading the Emancipation Proclamation to slaves

credit: Library of Congress

In the last week of 1862, newspapers predicted President Lincoln would renege on his promise to sign the Emancipation Proclamation on January 1, 1863.

Go to the link Visualizing Emancipation to find an interactive map of the United States. What was the relationship between the geography of a region and how early in the war enslaved people in this area became free?

 Richmond visualizing emancipation

TO ARMS, TO ARMS

As soon as Fort Sumter fell at the beginning of the war, free black men rushed to join the Union Army. They were rejected. A 1792 federal law barred blacks from serving in the militia. The Emancipation Proclamation changed this. African Americans were permitted to enlist in all branches of the armed services. Eventually, 179,000 black men served in the U.S. Army and another 19,000 served in the U.S. Navy.

However, the armed services did not treat African Americans equally. All-black regiments were led by white officers, and black troops were paid only $10 a month, compared to a white soldier's $13. Some soldiers protested by refusing their pay. In June 1864, Congress granted equal pay to all soldiers.

Some white soldiers hated the idea of arming African Americans. But many men changed their minds when they witnessed the courage of their black comrades. At first, Elisha Hunt Rhodes opposed arming blacks. But on June 19, 1864, he fought with a regiment of U.S. Colored Troops outside of Petersburg, Virginia. The next day, Rhodes wrote, "Yesterday's work convinced me that they will fight. So Hurrah for the colored troops!" However, even with the addition of black soldiers, the war was devouring men at a rapid pace.

An African-American soldier and his family

credit: Library of Congress

RIOTS

Dead soldiers must be replaced with live ones, so the U.S. Congress passed the Enrollment Act in March 1863. Single men between 20 and 45 and married men up to age 35 were eligible for the draft. Any man who did not want to fight could hire a substitute for $300. The wealthy could buy their way out of war, but the poor could not.

Draft resistance sprung up in Kentucky, New Hampshire, and Wisconsin, but was most violent in New York City. Working-class Irish immigrants resented being forced to fight a war to free slaves. On a muggy Monday in July, a mob attacked the draft office and set it ablaze. They looted the armory, jewelry shops, and liquor stores. By nightfall, mobs on the Upper East Side overpowered the police.

Rioters had three targets—the police, the Union Army, and the city's African Americans. A black orphanage was burned and roving bands ransacked black neighborhoods.

Lincoln refused to let the riots interfere with his need for manpower. "Time is too important," he said, and ordered Union troops to suppress the riot. It took five days to settle the city. Although the official death toll was 119, other estimates put it closer to 1,000. The draft continued.

While Northern men rioted to avoid the draft, Southern women rioted because they could not feed their children. The Rebel Army was authorized to seize crops and livestock. Farmers were compensated with Confederate money not worth the paper it was printed on. Many farmers stopped growing crops, and the price of goods skyrocketed. A monthly bill for a Confederate family's food was $6.65 in 1861. By 1863, it had jumped to $68.

The women of Richmond finally snapped. On April 2, 1863, they stormed through downtown, smashing windows and looting stores. President Davis raced to the scene. He threw a handful of coins into the crowd of angry women. "You say you are hungry and have no money," he shouted. "Here is all I have." Then Davis ordered them to leave before soldiers opened fire. The rioters straggled home.

RATION OF TRUTH

Regarding African-American soldiers, President Lincoln said, "There will be some black men who can remember that, with silent tongue, and clenched teeth, and steady eye, and well-poised bayonet, they have helped mankind on to this great consummation."

A field hospital at Gettysburg

credit: Library of Congress

THE CROSSROADS OF WAR

The sooner the Rebel Army struck a major blow to the Union, the sooner the war would end. Determined to achieve this, General Lee once again turned north in the summer of 1863. At the little town of Gettysburg, Pennsylvania, two great armies would meet in the pivotal battle of the Civil War.

This turning point began on July 1 with a skirmish between Confederate divisions and Union cavalry on the rolling fields around town. At the end of the day, Union troops controlled Culp's and Cemetery Hills, high ground that gave them the advantage.

By the next morning, 70,000 Confederates and 93,000 Union soldiers had gathered for battle. The Union front was a fish-hook shape, with Culp's and Cemetery Hills on the right and Little Round Top on the left. Lee attacked the entire line and almost broke through. But when dusk fell, federal troops still held the high ground.

The third day of battle dawned. Lee was convinced one strong charge into the Union's center would succeed. The war could be settled here and now. General James Longstreet strongly disagreed. "I have been a soldier all my life," he told Lee. "There are no 15,000 men in the world that can go across that ground."

But Lee's mind was made up. He pointed at Cemetery Ridge, where Union troops waited. "There is the enemy and there I mean to attack him."

At 1 in the afternoon, General Longstreet prepared to follow Lee's order. Confederate artillery bombarded the Union position ahead of the charge, and Union guns answered back. Longstreet rode before his line of soldiers, urging them to be brave as shells exploded around him. George Pickett, the young general chosen to lead the charge, requested permission to advance. Filled with emotion, Longstreet could only nod and turn away.

> He knew these brave boys were going to the slaughter.

Longstreet was right. Federal troops waited until the Rebels were close and then opened fire. Almost every shot hit its mark, some bullets killing several men at once. Almost half of Pickett's 13,000 men were dead, wounded, or taken prisoner.

The Confederates withdrew to a ridge and the battle ended. The next day, July 4, the Rebels slowly retreated south. General George Meade, the Union commander, did not pursue them. Lincoln was furious. He continued to search for a commander with the stomach to hammer the Rebels until they surrendered. He found such a man in Ulysses S. Grant.

A digital map from *Smithsonian Magazine* reveals how modern technology would have given commanders a different perspective during the Battle of Gettysburg. How might today's technology have altered the outcome of this battle?

 Smithsonian second look Gettysburg

RATION OF TRUTH

President Lincoln wrote a letter to General George Meade but never sent it, saying, "He was within your easy grasp, and to have closed upon him would . . . have ended the war—As it is, the war will be prolonged indefinitely."

MY MAN GRANT

Native Americans called the mighty Mississippi River the "Father of Waters." It cut through the center of the Confederacy, so control of the Mississippi was vital for a Union victory. But the city of Vicksburg, Mississippi, was in the Union's way.

Vicksburg sat high on the river bluffs and seemed impregnable. The Union Navy failed to take the city by water, so while Meade was engaging Confederate troops at Gettysburg, Lincoln ordered General Grant to seize Vicksburg by land. Grant led his army across the river, deep into enemy territory. Grants' troops marched 180 miles and fought five battles before reaching Vicksburg from the rear.

A 47-day siege followed. Union guns pounded the city from the water and land. Residents sheltered in hillside caves. The diseases of dysentery and malaria spread. Starving citizens ate rats and horses as supplies ran out.

Finally, the Confederates surrendered, and federal forces occupied Vicksburg on July 4, 1863. President Lincoln was overjoyed. He had found a general who could deliver a decisive victory. "Grant is my man," Lincoln said, "and I am his, for the rest of the war." The following spring, Lincoln named Grant commander in chief of all Union armies.

FRIED RAT

Sam Watkins had heard about people in Vicksburg, Mississippi, surviving on rats, so when Confederate forces in Tennessee ran low on rations in the fall of 1863, the men of Company H were hungry enough to give it a try. When they caught an old gray rat, its tail broke off in Watkins' hand. The soldiers skinned the rat and fried it up with salt and pepper. Watkins put a slice of meat on cornbread and raised it to his mouth. Suddenly, an image of the tail in his hand sprang into Watkins' mind. "I . . . lost my appetite . . . . It was my first and last effort to eat dead rats."

KEY QUESTIONS

- How did the Emancipation Proclamation change the outlook of soldiers and civilians on both sides of the war?

- What are some of the ways technological advances have altered the way wars play out?

GETTYSBURG ADDRESS

The telegraph was the Twitter of the nineteenth century, and Lincoln mastered this form of communication. Through the telegraph system, he could both wield control over distant battlefields and keep his finger on the pulse of the nation. Lincoln's powerful and concise language is best seen in the Gettysburg Address. Extract Lincoln's central point in this speech and communicate it like a master of twenty-first-century social media—in a tweet.

- **Locate a copy of the Gettysburg Address, in print or online.** You can find a transcript at this site.

 Gettysburg Address Avalon

- **Closely read the speech to identify who Lincoln's audience was.** Why was he making the speech? What was the main idea Lincoln wanted his audience to understand?

- **Write a tweet that sums up this main idea.** Tweets can only have 140 characters, including #hashtags.

To investigate more, contrast Lincoln's language in the Gettysburg Address with the Emancipation Proclamation. Which is easier to understand? Why? What are some explanations for why Lincoln used such a different style when writing these two documents? Compose a tweet that accurately communicates the main idea of the Emancipation Proclamation.

VOCAB LAB

Write down what you think each word means. What root words can you find to help you? What does the context of the word tell you?

bondage, colonization, immigrant, impregnable, pivotal, proclamation, prolonged, renege, skirmish, and **technology.**

Compare your definitions with those of your friends or classmates. Did you all come up with the same meanings? Turn to the text and glossary if you need help.

Suggested Supplies ▼

- friends or classmates
- batch of salt dough (the recipe can be found in craft books or online)
- large piece of cardboard
- plastic knife
- paints of various colors
- broken twigs or other small objects you can use to portray trees
- map pins or toy soldiers or other markers you can use to portray Union and Confederate commanders

GEOGRAPHY AS DESTINY

In the Battle of Gettysburg, about 165,000 soldiers fought on 6,000 acres of land. Investigate how geography impacted the outcome of this fight by making a three-dimensional battlefield map.

- **Research the key commanders of this battle.** Who were the important leaders on each side?

- **Mix up the salt dough.** Roll out enough to cover your cardboard base.

- **Consult maps of the Battle of Gettysburg.** The Library of Congress is a good place to find topographical maps and the Civil War Trust has easy-to-read maps that show water bodies, state borders, and troop movements.

 LOC Civil War maps   Civil War Trust maps

- **Add dough to make elevated areas.** Use the plastic knife or other tool to carve and form the natural and manmade features shown on the maps. Insert twigs to replicate heavily wooded areas.

- **Develop a key for your map.** Use colors and symbols to show the elevation of the land, as well as water bodies and roads.

- **Let the map dry for about one week.** When the dough is dry, paint the map according to your key.

- **Locate a good source that describes the Battle of Gettysburg.** While one person reads this account, two or more people move the markers to reenact the flow of the battle. Chart the key decisions commanders made, the geographical advantages or disadvantages they encountered during different phases of the battle, and the outcome of each decision.

- **Based on the data you gathered, how did geography impact the Battle of Gettysburg?** How did landforms, waterways, and manmade structures influence the flow or the outcome?

To investigate more, consider the concept of historical contingency, or the idea that events in history were not inevitable. The North was not destined to win the Civil War. Decisions were impacted by the landscape or the weather, things no one could have predicted. To explore the concept of historical contingency, review the command decisions listed on your chart and ask yourself, "What if?" Identify how different decisions by the commanders could have led to different outcomes.

To investigate more, design your own Civil War recruitment poster. Select whether you will recruit for the Union or the Confederacy, and decide if you want to design an ad to appeal to a broad range of people or a specific subgroup. When your poster is completed, ask friends or classmates to evaluate your work. Would your poster inspire them to fight?

RECRUITMENT POSTERS

Civil War recruitment posters enticed men to enlist in the Union and Confederate Armies. These advertisements made promises and appealed to peoples' patriotism. While some posters were designed for a broad audience, men were motivated to fight for different reasons. An Irish immigrant living in New York would probably not feel the same way as a free black man living in Wisconsin. A white man living in Massachusetts would not be inspired to enlist for the same reasons a white man living in Texas would. Analyze Civil War recruitment posters to determine what devices government artists used to appeal to these different groups.

- **Locate several copies of Union and Confederate recruitment posters online.** Good examples are at the Library of Congress "Civil War in America" online exhibit and under primary sources on the Gilder Lehrman website.

LOC Civil War April 1861– April 1862

Gilder Lehrman browse the collection Civil War recruitment posters

- **What words and images do these posters use to inspire feelings of patriotism?** What incentives are offered to volunteers? How are different racial or ethnic groups targeted specifically?

- **What do the posters tell you about the regiments doing the recruiting?** Are these posters effective tools? How could you make them more effective?

Chapter 6
The Scourge of War

MEN, I PROPOSE TOTAL WAR ON THE REBELS! WE WILL EAT THEIR FOOD, BURN THEIR SUPPLIES, AND MAKE THEM BEG.

Was General Sherman justified in his brutal actions in the South?

If General Sherman had not accomplished his march, during which many soldiers and civilians were harmed, the war might have continued for much longer. But some people believe he had no right to be so violent. What do you think?

On March 9, 1864, the president formally commissioned Ulysses S. Grant as general-in-chief of the U.S. Army. The generals who had preceded Grant all believed victory lay in the capture of Richmond. Grant disagreed. Capturing cities and occupying territory meant nothing if Confederate armies still lived to fight. Grant intended to destroy the Confederate Army so there would be no resistance left.

While Grant took on General Robert E. Lee and the Army of Northern Virginia, his second in command, General William Tecumseh Sherman (1820–1891), would strike General Joseph Johnston's Confederate forces in Georgia. The hope was that a comprehensive attack on multiple fronts would weaken the Confederate Army enough that it couldn't possibly rebound and the South would surrender.

OUT OF THE WILDERNESS

Spring flowers turned to ash when Grant and Lee met on the battlefield in Virginia in May 1864. Grant led his army across the Rapidan River into a stretch of woods known as the Wilderness. His aim was to get between Lee's army and Richmond. However, Lee anticipated Grant's move and attacked when federal troops were in the middle of the impenetrable forest. For two brutal days, the fighting raged. Gunpowder turned the woodlands into a sulfurous cauldron. Brush caught fire and more than 200 wounded men burned alive.

Battle of the Wilderness—Desperate fight on the Orange C.H. Plank Road, near Todd's Tavern, May 6, 1864

credit: Library of Congress

Despite the casualties, Grant did not retreat. The Battle of the Wilderness ended on May 7, 1864, and Union soldiers were ordered to march. The men assumed they were retreating back to Washington, DC, as they had done under every other commander. But when the army reached a crossroads, officers pointed south. "On to Richmond," the troops cried. General Grant appeared on horseback. The men cheered and tossed their hats, thankful they finally had a leader determined to fight hard enough to end the war.

For six long weeks, Grant and Lee tried to annihilate each other. After the battles of Spotsylvania and Cold Harbor, the Union Army reached Petersburg, Virginia, and settled in for a 10-month siege.

WOMEN'S WORK

The war brought both hardship and opportunity for American women. Some women leapt at the chance to fight the enemy. Historians estimate between 400 and 1,000 women disguised themselves as men and fought in the Civil War. After the bloody Battle of Fredericksburg, a corporal from New Jersey was promoted to sergeant. A comrade described this soldier as "a real soldierly, thoroughly military fellow." One month later, that sergeant gave birth to a baby boy.[1]

Because soldiers slept in fields, rarely bathed, and went months without changing their clothes while on the march, women could avoid detection. Female soldiers served for the same reasons as men— adventure, escape, and patriotism. Sarah Edmonds wrote in 1865 that she "could only thank God that I was free and could go forward and work, and I was not obliged to stay at home and weep."

Northern women uninterested in carrying guns found other ways to serve. Some joined the army as "daughters of the regiment," performing vital work for a relative's regiment, such as laundry, cooking, or medical care. Susie Baker King Taylor followed her husband's regiment of the U.S. Colored Troops, first as laundress and then as nurse. In her memoir, Taylor wrote that war toughed women up. "We are able to see the most sickening sights, such as men with their limbs blown off . . . and instead of turning away, how we hurry to . . . bind up their wounds . . . ."

> Before the Civil War, most army nurses were male.

Educator and activist Dorothea Dix (1802–1887) changed that after the secretary of war appointed her as the superintendent of female nurses of the Union Army. While not medically trained, Dix was a master organizer. She sought out women between the ages of 35 and 50, hoping to develop a skilled crew of mature nurses who were immune to romance. More than 3,000 of Dix's nurses served the Union during the war.

For Confederate women, the front line of battle often landed on their doorsteps. Carrie McGavock's Tennessee plantation was used as a field hospital after the Battle of Franklin on November 30, 1864. A Confederate general described the condition of McGavock's home in a letter. "Every room was filled, every bed had two poor, bleeding fellows, every spare space, niche, and corner under the stairs . . . ." Doctors ran low on bandages, so McGavock gave them cloth—first her towels and napkins, then sheets and tablecloths, and finally her own skirts.[2]

Frances Clalin Clayton, a woman who disguised herself as a man to fight for the Union Army

credit: Library of Congress

Read a newspaper article from *The Washington Post* about women on the Civil War battlefield.

 WaPo women soldiers Civil War

THE SCOURGE OF WAR

Amanda Akins (1827–1911) served as a nurse in the Armory Square Hospital in Washington, DC, for 15 months during the Civil War. Go to this site to read excerpts of her diary and see images of what she would have encountered in the capital.

🔍 diary of Civil War nurse

RATION OF TRUTH

Sherman wrote to Grant, "I would make this war as severe as possible and show no symptoms of tiring till the South begs for mercy."

For enslaved women in the South, the advance of the Union Army brought exhilaration and fear. Those who could ran to Union lines with their children in tow. Some found work as seamstresses or laundresses or even laborers with the military, but most eked out a living in contraband camps. They planted gardens and raised animals and endured abuse from soldiers, the threat of disease, and the uncertainty of life on the edge of a war zone.

TOTAL WAR

While Grant laid siege to Confederate forces outside of Petersburg, Virginia, General William Tecumseh Sherman marched through Georgia. Considered America's first modern general, Sherman was the first commander to implement the strategy of total war.

This meant any resources that would help the Confederacy continue to fight were targets—livestock, bridges, railroads, plantations—even if this property was owned by Southern civilians.

In May 1864, Sherman led an army of 100,000 into Georgia in pursuit of Rebels led by General Johnston. The fighting was fierce. At the Battle of Kennesaw Mountain on July 27, Sam Watkins endured the blazing fire of Yankee guns. He said, "Our tongues were parched and cracked for water, and our faces blackened with powder and smoke, and our dead and wounded were piled indiscriminately in the trenches."

President Jefferson Davis believed General Johnston lacked the will to win. In July, Davis replaced him with General John Bell Hood (1831–1879).

Confederate soldiers were stunned. Some soldiers threw down their guns when they heard of Johnston's removal. Some men even deserted.

Hood proved to be a poor replacement. Sherman's army backed the Rebels into Atlanta and began a five-week bombardment of the city. By the end of August 1864, Hood ordered his men to evacuate the city, leaving about 2,000 citizens who still lived in Atlanta.

Sherman ordered them out. "If the people raise a howl against my barbarity and cruelty, I will answer that war is war, and not popularity-seeking. If they want peace, they . . . must stop the war." The people left and Sherman set the city ablaze. All that remained of Atlanta were churches, city hall, and a few private houses.[3]

Atlanta was one of the Confederacy's most important cities, and it was now in Union hands. This victory saved Abraham Lincoln's presidency.

A political cartoon from 1864

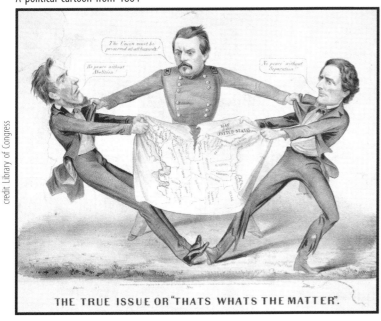

credit Library of Congress

THE TRUE ISSUE OR "THATS WHATS THE MATTER".

NO MERCY

Years after the war ended, Private Sam Watkins recalled Sherman's March with hostility as raw as if the war had ended yesterday. In his memoir, Watkins adopted the persona of a Rebel talking to a Yank.

"We are ready to play quits now," said the Reb . . . . "You can parole us . . . and we'll go home and be . . . good Union boys." . . .

"You are proud and aristocratic," replied the Yank. ". . . We are going to crush your cursed pride and spirit . . . . We ain't done with you yet, my boy . . . we want to rob and then burn every house in Georgia . . . ."

REELECTION

Prospects for reelection looked grim for Lincoln in 1864. His Democratic opponent was his former top commander, George McClellan. Northerners were war-weary and many had not supported the Emancipation Proclamation. Lincoln resigned himself to defeat.

When General Sherman captured Atlanta in September 1864, the political landscape shifted. The victory buoyed Northern spirits. Strife within the Democratic Party confused its message. McClellan claimed peace was impossible until the Rebels rejoined the nation, but other Democrats insisted peace must come before reunification. Union troops overwhelmingly supported Lincoln.

Lincoln won a decisive victory, earning 212 electoral votes out of a possible 233. The news of Lincoln's victory was a death knell for the Confederacy. There would be no peace negotiations. The South must surrender.

MARCH TO THE SEA

With Atlanta in Union hands, Sherman looked farther east. He wanted to march through 225 miles of Georgia countryside to the city of Savannah. Grant and Lincoln were skeptical. They feared that unless Sherman destroyed John Bell Hood's army, Hood could march on Tennessee.

But Sherman's plan was part of his total war strategy. His army would live off the land as they marched, taking crops and livestock from civilians. Grant gave Sherman the go-ahead. On November 16, 1864, Sherman's army of 62,000 left Atlanta, heading southeast.

FORT PILLOW

The Confederate Congress refused to treat captured black troops equally. After the Emancipation Proclamation, it vowed to enslave any captured African-American soldier. Some commanders went farther. At the Battle of Fort Pillow in April 1864, Confederate General Nathan Bedford Forrest did not stop his troops from massacring close to 300 Union soldiers—most of whom were African American—after they had surrendered.

Go to the Library of Congress website to view a painting of Sherman's March. How would the actions of the Union Army shown in this painting hurt the Confederate war effort?

 LOC Sherman's March

An elite group of foragers, known as "bummers," moved alongside the flanks of the army. The bummers confiscated vegetables, livestock, and horse feed. Some men roughed up Confederate citizens and ransacked their houses, stealing jewelry, silver, and other treasures. Sherman estimated his army took 5,000 cattle, 2,500 wagons, and 15,000 mules from Southern citizens. Union troops destroyed Rebel rail lines by prying up railroad ties, heating the iron, and twisting them around trees. The troops called these Sherman neckties. The March to the Sea was a military success.

> But Sherman's total war strategy left a bitter taste in the mouths of white Southerners that would last a generation.

On December 22, 1864, General Sherman sent a letter to President Lincoln. "I beg to present you as a Christmas gift the City of Savannah . . . ." The year was ending. Victory was within the grasp of the Union. It was up to General Ulysses S. Grant to seize it.[4]

VOCAB LAB

Write down what you think each word means. What root words can you find to help you? What does the context of the word tell you?

annihilate, **comprehensive**, **contraband**, **desertion**, **electoral vote**, **forager**, **impenetrable**, and **total war strategy**.

Compare your definitions with those of your friends or classmates. Did you all come up with the same meanings? Turn to the text and glossary if you need help.

KEY QUESTIONS

- **How might the outcome of the war been different if Lincoln had lost the presidency?**
- **Was it right for General Sherman to be so brutal in his treatment of the South? Do the ends justify the means?**
- **Can you think of other times in history when a brutal action brought about a dramatic change in a conflict?**

Suggested Supplies ▼

- aluminum cake pans to catch soil runoff
- aluminum bread pans to serve as earth fortifications
- topsoil to fill bread pans
- scale to measure soil runoff
- fast-growing seeds such as radishes, bush beans, or marigolds
- plastic container to create a hill

To investigate more, consider how real-world situations might compare and contrast with the conditions in your experiment. What other land-management strategies is the National Park Service using to prevent soil erosion on Civil War battlefield fortifications?

STOP THE EROSION OF HISTORY

The basic earthen fort used for defense by both sides in the Civil War consisted of a parapet, or mound of earth, and a ditch. The National Park Service is charged with preserving Civil War battlefields. One of the biggest challenges it faces is soil erosion of earthen fortifications. Wind and rain move soil, but so do the feet of thousands of history-loving humans. Perform an experiment to determine whether plants can prevent soil erosion.

- **Design an experiment to test the effectiveness of different plants in preventing soil erosion.** Consider how you can create a slope to represent the parapet and ditch structure of Civil War fortifications.

  - How can you prevent water from building up in the bottom of the bread pans when you use the watering can to make it "rain"?

  - How will you guarantee that the height of the slope is the same for each earth fortification you build?

  - What technique will you use to make it rain evenly on the entire earth fort, rather than in just one spot?

  - How will you ensure an equal amount of rain falls on each earth fort?

- **Graph your results.** Look at your data and determine the conclusion of your investigation. Do hillsides with plants safeguard the soil better than a bare hillside? Does one type of plant perform better than the rest? If so, what makes the structure of that plant more effective at holding in the soil?

Chapter 7 ▶
One and Undivided

WELL, THE WAR IS OVER. I SPENT THE LAST 3 YEARS FIGHTING...NOW WHAT?

How does a nation so bitterly divided handle the end of the conflict?

The Union finally crushed the Confederacy, forcing it to surrender. But that wasn't the end of ill feelings on both sides of the conflict.

By the beginning of 1865, the Confederacy was in its final days. The South struggled to feed its prisoners of war and its own soldiers. General Lee failed in his final attempt to break out of General Grant's pincers, and finally surrendered on April 9, 1865. But the ink of the ceasefire was barely dry when the nation faced another great challenge.

On April 14, President Abraham Lincoln was assassinated. The man who had led a divided nation back to unity was dead. The war had caused so much death and destruction. Many Southerners still believed deeply in the cause for which they had fought. How would this newly reunified nation handle the blow of Lincoln's murder while trying to heal from the wounds of war?

CITY OF DEATH

In southern Georgia, a wooden stockade enclosed 26 acres of land. Inside this pen ran a branch of Sweetwater Creek. By the summer of 1864, the water had long lost all sweetness. The sewage of thousands of Union prisoners polluted the stream, from which the prisoners also drank. Originally constructed for only 10,000, Andersonville Prison Camp held 33,000 Yankee soldiers at its peak. Their struggle for survival was the stuff of nightmares.

A narrow strip of board nailed to 4-foot-high stakes ran the inner circuit of the prison stockade. This "deadline" was about 20 feet from the wall where guards stood posted. Any prisoner who touched the deadline was shot.

Go to the National Park Service website to view a collection of photographs of Union soldiers taken after the Andersonville Prison Camp was liberated. What do these pictures reveal about the prison camp's conditions and the resources of the Confederacy by the end of the Civil War?

Warning: These images might be disturbing for some viewers.

NPS prisoner photographs

Andersonville Prison Camp

credit: Library of Congress

At 10 each morning, a drum roll signaled the arrival of the ration wagon. The prisoners lined up in detachments of 90 men. Confederate sergeants were charged with counting each detachment, and the Yankee prisoners were forced to stand during the long tally. Men who had died overnight were hauled away.

The rations for a 24-hour period included a thin square of cornbread and a piece of bacon.

BLACKS IN THE CONFEDERATE ARMY

On March 23, 1865, the Confederate Congress passed an emancipation bill that would grant freedom to slaves who volunteered to fight in the Rebel Army. Only 50 slaves signed on. After the war, a journalist asked a few if they would have actually fought for the South. One man said the Rebels could have shot him with "ninety-thousand balls" before he would have fired a shot in their defense. Another claimed he would have grabbed a gun, shot the Rebels, and then ran for Union lines. The war ended before any African-American Rebels were tested in battle.

Prisoners became walking skeletons. One soldier suffered from scurvy so badly that gangrene settled in his feet. His only hope for survival was amputation, but prisoners did not receive medical care from their captors and none of the other prisoners had the stomach to perform the surgery. So the man sawed off his own feet.

One morning in July 1864, Sam Watkins' regiment was ordered to board a train from Atlanta toward Andersonville. General Sherman had given permission for General George Stoneman and his cavalry brigade to attempt a rescue of the Yankee prisoners of war (POWs). Watkins was sent to try to prevent this rescue.

Stoneman's men rode ahead of the Confederate train. Every few miles, they tore up a section of railroad track. Watkins' train drove at breakneck speed, but then was forced to screech to a halt while the broken track was repaired.

The Union rescue still failed, and Stoneman and his cavalry were taken prisoners themselves. Watkins boasted in his memoirs that these Yanks had "Furnished their own transportation, [paid] their own way and [bore] their own expenses" all the way to prison. Andersonville would not be liberated until after the war ended. But that day was fast approaching.

FINAL DAYS

Meanwhile, General Grant's siege of Petersburg, Virginia, continued. As the months rolled on, the line of Confederates defending Petersburg thinned while the Union line thickened. Grant mounted a massive assault on the city on April 2, 1865. As Federals poured into the city, Lee gave the order to evacuate. He fled with the remains of the Army of Northern Virginia, but Grant was hot on his heels.

The Confederate government had sent out peace feelers in early 1865. On February 3, Confederate Vice President Alexander Stephens met President Lincoln and Secretary of State William Seward on a federal steamboat at Hampton Roads, Virginia. The conversation went nowhere.

Lincoln said the war would end only when the Rebel army disbanded, when the Confederacy recognized the national government of the United States, and when slavery was abolished. Jefferson Davis vowed to fight on.

A few weeks later, on March 4, 1865, a crowd braved the cold rain to watch Abraham Lincoln take the oath of office for a second time. As he stepped forward to speak, the sun broke through the clouds.

"Fellow countrymen," Lincoln began," . . . if God wills that [the war] continue until . . . every drop of blood drawn with the lash shall be paid by another drawn with the sword . . . the judgments of the Lord are true and righteous . . . ." He was reminding people that centuries of slavery carried a price.

But Lincoln ended his address on a friendly note. "With malice toward none, with charity for all . . . let us strive on to finish the work we are in; to bind up the nation's wounds . . . and cherish a just and a lasting peace . . . ."[1]

WE ARE ALL AMERICANS

Throughout the early nineteenth century, Native Americans endured racial discrimination and forced relocation to reservation lands. Perhaps hoping that military service would lead to full citizenship rights, roughly 20,000 Native Americans fought on both sides in the Civil War. But justice for Native Americans did not come to pass. Following the Civil War, the railroad was extended westward and white settlers followed. Native Americans suffered through more wars, massacres, and land seizures.

President Lincoln's second inauguration

credit: Alexander Gardner, Library of Congress

Following the inauguration, Lincoln fell ill. From what is unclear, but he said, "I'm a tired man. Sometimes, I think I'm the tiredest man on earth."

LEE'S LAST GASP

On April 2, 1865, Jefferson Davis was attending church in Richmond when he was handed a message. A gray pallor spread across his face as he read it. The Union Army was outside the city, and General Lee could not defend it. The time had come to evacuate the capital. Davis and his cabinet fled Richmond by train while the city plunged into chaos. People pillaged liquor warehouses. The Confederate Army destroyed its ironclad ships in the James River and blew up four tobacco warehouses.

Flames licked onto neighboring buildings and the city caught fire. As the Union Army entered Richmond, it tried to quench the flames, but as night fell, many buildings became charred ruins. People slept in the shadows of the Confederate capital as bells in Washington chimed victoriously.

Lee marched his exhausted soldiers south to connect with General Johnston's army. But Union General Philip Sheridan cut him off, forcing the Rebels west. Their situation was dire. The Confederate government was on the run. The army was out of rations, and the Union cavalry steadily harassed the troops as the Confederates marched.

President Davis set up new headquarters in a private home in Danville, Virginia. On April 4, he issued his final proclamation as president. Davis urged his countrymen not to quit.

> He called on the citizens of the South to "let us meet the foe with fresh defiance, with unconquered and unconquerable hearts."

Davis was proposing guerrilla warfare. But the president was no longer calling the shots for the Confederacy. General Lee was.

SURRENDER AT APPOMATTOX

Union forces surrounded the Rebels at the small town of Appomattox Court House. The evening of April 8, 1865, Lee and his generals had their final war council. They agreed—they were trapped. "There is nothing left me," Lee said, "but to go and see General Grant, and I had rather die a thousand deaths."

You can read the letters and speeches of Jefferson Davis at the Rice University website. Do you think he had regrets about his role in the Civil War?

 Rice Jefferson Davis

The burning of Richmond, Virginia

BURNING AND EVACUATION OF RICHMOND APRIL 3RD 1865.

credit: Library of Congress

The surrender of General Lee (right) to General Grant at Appomattox Court House by Thomas Nast

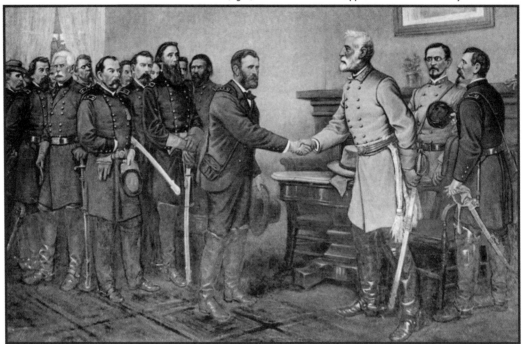

The next morning, Grant was riding a circuit around his army. He'd had a migraine for 24 hours, and he hoped fresh air would blow it away. While Grant was on his ride, an aide galloped up, a message from General Lee in his hand. Grant read the note and immediately sat down on the ground. Lee wanted to surrender. The aide said Grant exhibited no more emotion than "last year's bird nest." However, Lee's message was exactly what Grant needed. His migraine vanished.

A short time later, the generals met in the parlor of a local home. Grant, who came straight from his ride, was dusty and dressed in "rough garb." By contrast, Lee had donned a new dress uniform and a jewel-hilted sword dangled from his belt. The men shook hands and got down to business.

Lincoln had authorized Grant to offer a "tender peace" with generous terms. Confederate officers could keep their sidearms and private property. Because most Rebel soldiers were farmers, enlisted men could keep any horse they owned. Lee asked for any rations Grant could spare. The Rebels had been living on dry corn for days.

After the agreement was signed, Grant introduced Lee to his staff. When Lee shook hands with Grant's military secretary, Ely Parker, who was a Seneca Indian, Lee said, "I am glad to see at least one real American here." Parker replied, "We are all Americans."[2]

The surrender was an emotional moment for both Grant and Lee. Grant later wrote, "I felt like anything rather than rejoicing at the downfall of a foe who had fought so long and valiantly . . . ." As Lee rode back to Confederate lines, his men rushed to shake his hand and touch his horse.

> The general could hardly speak. "Men, we have fought through the war together. I have done the best I could for you. My heart is too full to say more."

When Lee returned to camp, a group of soldiers waited outside his tent. This was a critical moment. If Lee had ordered his troops to take to the hills and mount a guerilla warfare campaign, they would have obeyed. However, the general told his soldiers it was time to go home, and, "if you make as good citizens as you have soldiers, you will do well, and I shall always be proud of you." This was Robert E. Lee's gift to the nation.

GENERAL LEE'S SURRENDER

"After four years of arduous service marked by unsurpassed courage and fortitude, the Army of Northern Virginia has been compelled to yield to overwhelming numbers and resources." Lee stated his official surrender in his General Order No. 9 signed on April 10, 1865.

Go to this site to read the entire document. What reason does he give for surrendering?

General Lee surrender

Grant's surrender terms were also a gift to the country. If the Rebels surrendered their arms and lived up to the terms of their parole, the federal government would not bother them. No one would be executed for treason. Grant spared the nation the pain of drawn-out trials and hangings.

On the ride back to field headquarters, Grant dismounted and scribbled a quick note to President Lincoln. "General Lee surrendered the Army of Northern Virginia this afternoon . . . ." When he received the note, Lincoln sank to his knees in prayer.

Elisha Hunt Rhodes was with the army at Appomattox. About midday, he heard a cheering from the front lines. Major General Meade appeared on horseback, galloping down the road with hat in hand. "The war is over, and we are going home!" Meade cried. Rhodes said the troops "threw their knapsacks and canteens into the air and howled . . . ."

Three days later, the official surrender ceremony occurred. Confederate soldiers turned in their rifles one by one. Both armies faced each other. Union soldiers were led by Joshua Lawrence Chamberlain, hero of the Battle of Gettysburg. General John B. Gordon commanded the Confederates. He had been shot five times in Bloody Lane at the Battle of Antietam. Chamberlain barked an order, and the Union soldiers shifted their guns in a salute to their former enemies. The Army of Northern Virginia ceased to exist.

When the news reached Washington, fireworks lit the sky and a crowd gathered around the White House. President Lincoln appeared briefly and asked the band to play "Dixie." The song that had served as an unofficial Confederate anthem was once again for all Americans.

CITIZENSHIP RESTORED

Following the war, senior Confederate officers had to apply for pardons in order to restore their citizenship. General Robert E. Lee completed such an application on June 13, 1865. His request was never processed, however. In 1970, a worker at the National Archives discovered Lee's application buried among other records. President Gerald Ford pardoned Lee in 1975, 105 years after his death.

On April 14, four years to the day that Fort Sumter fell to the Confederates, the stars and stripes flew once again over the island. Major Robert Anderson, the commander who had surrendered the fort in 1861, raised "the old smoke-stained, shot-pierced flag" and thanked God he had lived to see this day.

THE DEATH OF LINCOLN

That same evening, President Lincoln and his wife headed out to celebrate by attending a play. From a private box at Ford's Theater, Lincoln chuckled to the punch lines in *Our American Cousin*. His single bodyguard, an unreliable police officer, had entered the gallery to watch the play.

RATION OF TRUTH

Explore *National Geographic*'s interactive site on the assassination of President Lincoln at Killinglincoln. nationalgeographic.com. What was required for such a conspiracy to be successful? Was it successful?

 National Geographic killing Lincoln

The assassination of President Lincoln

credit: Library of Congress

THE ASSASSINATION OF PRESIDENT LINCOLN,
AT FORD'S THEATRE WASHINGTON, D.C. APRIL 14TH 1865.

PRESIDENT JEFFERSON DAVIS

President Jefferson Davis was also on the run from authorities. On May 9, he was camped with his family and staff near Irwinville, Georgia. Before dawn, 128 mounted soldiers surrounded the camp. Davis tried to make a run for it, but was captured. Jefferson Davis spent two years in prison at Fort Monroe, Virginia. Never tried for treason, he was released on bond in 1867. Davis continued to insist the South's secession was justified and refused to request a pardon. The former Confederate president never regained his citizenship and spent the rest of his life as a man without a country.

Actor and Confederate sympathizer John Wilkes Booth slipped silently into the unguarded presidential box. Waiting until the auditorium was ringing with laughter, Booth drew his pistol and shot Lincoln in the back of the head. As the president collapsed and Mary Todd Lincoln screamed, Booth vaulted over the edge of the box, landing on the stage floor. Despite a broken leg, he hobbled offstage and out of the theater to his waiting horse. Booth rode like the wind for Virginia.

Lincoln, unconscious and bleeding, was carried to a boardinghouse across the street. A physician examined the president. The bullet had entered the back of his skull and was lodged in his brain. Death was soon to follow.

As officials and family gathered around Lincoln's bedside, they learned other assassins had been at work in the city. Booth's accomplice, Lewis Powell, also known as Lewis Paine, had stabbed Secretary of State Seward, critically wounding him. Another co-conspirator, George Atzerodt, was supposed to assassinate Vice President Andrew Johnson, but lost his nerve.

At 7:22 a.m. the next day, on Saturday, April 15, 1865, Abraham Lincoln took his last breath.

When Elisha Hunt Rhodes and his fellow soldiers heard the president had been assassinated, they were stunned and angry. "[We] are wild with rage to think that this great and good man who did so much for our land should be stricken down in the hour of victory." Lincoln's body traveled by funeral train to Springfield, Illinois, mourners lining the tracks in every town along the route.

A manhunt began. On April 26, Booth was discovered hiding in a barn in Virginia. During capture, he was shot and killed. In the frenzy following Lincoln's murder, many suspected Southern sympathizers were rounded up and held without trial. Ultimately, seven men and one woman were speedily tried and convicted. Four received life sentences and four were hanged.

Although the surrender of the Army of Northern Virginia signaled the war was over, fighting continued for several more weeks. On April 26, 1865, General Joseph Johnston gave up, signaling the end of fighting for Sam Watkins.

When his 1st Tennessee Regiment unit had formed in 1861, it had between 1,167 and 2,099 men. The day they surrendered, Watkins was one of 125 soldiers left alive. Watkins had no regrets for the role he played in the war, although he did "mourn the loss of so many brave and gallant men who perished on the field of battle and honor."

The Civil War was over, but its influence on America culture would extend far past the dates of surrender. Even today, American citizens feel the lingering effects of their country's bloodiest war.

VOCAB LAB

Write down what you think each word means. What root words can you find to help you? What does the context of the word tell you?

accomplice, **anthem**, **circuit**, **discrimination**, **gangrene**, **guerrilla warfare**, **justice**, **massacre**, **migraine**, **pardon**, **pillage**, **POW**, **relocation**, **scurry**, and **treason**.

Compare your definitions with those of your friends or classmates. Did you all come up with the same meanings? Turn to the text and glossary if you need help.

KEY QUESTIONS

- **Why do you think General Grant made the terms of surrender so agreeable to the Confederacy?**
- **How did Lincoln's assassination affect the aftermath of the Civil War?**

DESIGN A HUMANE POW CAMP

On April 24, 1863, President Lincoln issued General Orders No. 100. More commonly known as the Lieber Code, this order told Union officials how to conduct themselves during war. One section provided instructions about the humane treatment of POWs. Read that section of the code to understand what protections must be provided for prisoners. With the hindsight of history, design a humane prison camp for Andersonville, Georgia.

• **Research Andersonville Prison Camp to learn what mistakes were made when designing this camp.** Camp blueprints are located at the Library of Congress website.

> LOC plan Andersonville

• **Brainstorm the physical, social, and personal needs a Civil War prisoner would have.** Consider how you will meet these needs.

• **What questions must be answered before beginning your design?** Consider the following.

  • How many prisoners will Andersonville hold?

  • What is the geography of the building site?

  • What is the climate of this region?

  • How long will the prisoners be housed?

  • How much water and how many calories does an average person need per day?

  • How much fuel will be required for cooking, heating, and lighting?

• **Compile your answers to these questions into a report.** How could you present it to an inspector from the War Department?

• **Use the data you have gathered to draw a blueprint of an improved Andersonville Prison Camp.** What is different from the original camp?

To investigate more, consider that the Union POW camp in Elmira, New York, was a deadly place for Confederate prisoners. How did the conditions in Elmira compare to those of Andersonville? Were there any model POW camps during the Civil War?

Chapter 8 ▶
Legacies

THEY SAY WE ARE FREE, BUT THIS SHARECROPPING ISN'T MUCH BETTER.

How did the lives of African Americans change after the Civil War ended?

One aim of Reconstruction was to give full citizenship rights to African Americans. Because of political maneuvering on the part of the nation's new president and seething resentment and bigotry still present in the country, a decade after the Civil War ended, blacks still found themselves enslaved in many ways.

On July 7, 1865, Elisha Hunt Rhodes received orders to "muster out" his troops. The long war had ended, and it was time to go home. Rhodes had waited for this moment for years. "No more suffering, no more scenes of carnage and death," he wrote in his diary. "Thank God it is over and that the Union is restored."

Rhodes was one of the lucky ones. Four years of war killed a generation of American men. More than 620,000 soldiers died—360,000 Yankees and 260,000 Rebels.

THE AFTERMATH

At war's end, the chasm between the North and South was deep. The economy was booming in the North. Industrial production and efficiency hit new highs as factories turned out rifles, bullets, uniforms, and tents. Northern farms grew surpluses of wheat, corn, pork, and wool.

The picture was much grimmer in the South. Southern cities such as Fredericksburg and Atlanta lay in rubble. Weeds overran fields. Two-fifths of the South's livestock was killed during the war. Railroad and riverboat services were inoperable. Confederate soldiers who survived often returned home missing an arm or a leg.

In 1866 alone, one-fifth of Mississippi's state budget was spent on artificial limbs for veterans.

Slavery was over. The plantation economy was destroyed. The entire Southern economy would have to be rebuilt. In 1860, the South's slaves were worth $3.5 billion. The value for slave owners was now zero, because these enslaved people were now free.

GAINS FOR AFRICAN AMERICANS

Frederick Douglass knew that once African Americans were allowed to join the military, they would demand more when the war ended. In 1863, he wrote, "Once let the black man get upon his person the brass letters U.S., let him get an eagle on his button, and a musket on his shoulder, and bullets in his pocket, and there is no power on earth or under the earth which can deny that he has earned the right of citizenship in the United States."

Douglass was right. Following the war, African Americans embraced their newfound freedom. Families torn apart by slavery searched for each other. One Northern reporter interviewed a black man who walked 600 miles searching for his wife and children. Couples who had lived as husband and wife in slavery got married legally.

African Americans voting in New Orleans, Louisiana, in 1867

credit: New York Public Library Digital Collections

You can read about the experiences of African Americans following the Civil War and see pictures of some of the challenges they faced at this website. Why was education such a important part of gaining equality?

Reconstruction black community

New York Public Library has images of Reconstruction. What do these sketches reveal about gains made by blacks during this era?

 NYPL Reconstruction images

RATION OF TRUTH

In an 1863 speech, Andrew Johnson, the man who would become president when Abraham Lincoln was assassinated, said, "I am for this government with slavery under the Constitution as it is . . . . Before I would see this government destroyed, I would send every Negro back to Africa . . . ."

Long forced to worship in secret or in the back of white-run churches, African Americans now pooled their resources to build their own churches. These houses of worship became the center of new black communities.

Under slavery, blacks had been forbidden to learn how to read. Hungry to learn, black communities constructed schools for their children and staffed them with black teachers. The first black universities were also founded at this time.

African Americans held "colored citizen" conventions to demand rights not granted by the end of the war. At a convention in Norfolk, Virginia, on June 5, 1865, delegates wrote an appeal to "The People of the United States." They listed the ways former Confederates were abusing and discriminating against blacks in Virginia. Delegates asked their fellow Americans to "give us the suffrage, and you may rely upon us to secure justice for ourselves." With the power to vote, blacks knew they could change America.

Some whites argued that former slaves lacked the education to vote. African Americans rejected this. At one convention a man insisted, "If we don't know enough to know what the Constitution is, we know enough to know what justice is." Such appeals for justice were written at black conventions across the country.[1]

African Americans in the North also agitated for equality. Michigan men petitioned the state legislature to abolish laws referencing skin color. In Illinois, people worked to repeal a law banning African Americans from moving to the state. The target in California was a law that forbade blacks to testify against whites. In Philadelphia, blacks integrated the streetcars.

White backlash was fierce. In the South, 33 major race riots occurred. Violence erupted when white mobs broke up black political meetings or interfered with their efforts to vote.

THE POLITICS OF RECONSTRUCTION

In March 1865, shortly before the war ended, Congress created the Freedmen's Bureau. This federal agency provided food, housing, medical aid, education, and legal assistance to former slaves. But the Freedmen's Bureau existed for only one year, because with Lincoln's death, a new president was in charge—Andrew Johnson.

A Democrat from Tennessee, Johnson had been chosen as Lincoln's running mate in 1864 to prove Republicans wanted unity. When the presidency passed to Johnson, Reconstruction became his responsibility. However, Johnson's views on African Americans did not match that of congressional Republicans.

Johnson had opposed secession, but he also did not believe in equality for African Americans. Congress was not in session when Johnson assumed the presidency, so he quickly went to work reconstructing the South according to his own vision.

Former Confederate states were required to write new state constitutions that made slavery and secession illegal. Once these constitutions were approved, the states could elect members to Congress. Before a Southerner could vote, he must swear a loyalty oath to the U.S. government, and former Confederate politicians and high-ranking officers had to apply to Johnson for a pardon.

RACE RIOT

On July 30, 1866, more than 100 African-American delegates marched the streets of New Orleans to the site of the Louisiana's Constitutional Convention. A mob of ex-Confederates and city police attacked the marchers, who rushed inside the building for safety. The mob circled the building and opened fire. Blacks who surrendered were shot on the spot. Violence spread and, by the end of the day, 44 African Americans had been killed and more than 100 injured.

On paper, these reforms looked good, but in practice they led to former Confederates regaining political power throughout the South. President Johnson handed out pardons like candy, granting 7,000 by 1866. The Southern states elected many former Confederate leaders to Congress. The citizens of Georgia even chose Alexander Stephens, the former vice president of the Confederacy, as their new senator. The idea that these men would sit in the halls of the U.S. Congress galled citizens of the North.

Even worse, Southern states created "black codes" to replace the old slave codes. African Americans could not own guns, gather after dark, or marry whites. Blacks who did not have a job could be arrested for vagrancy and auctioned off to a planter to work for a year without pay. Former slaves could not buy land. Many became sharecroppers on land owned by their former slave owners. How could this be considered freedom?

When Congress returned from recess in December 1865, Republicans quickly tried to undo Johnson's actions. Northerners supported this reversal because no one wanted the war to have been fought for nothing. For a brief period, the rights of African Americans expanded and real freedom was finally within their reach.

EXPANSION OF CIVIL RIGHTS

Radical Reconstruction lasted from 1866 to 1877. During this era, Congress tried to safeguard former slaves through both legislation and amendments to the U.S. Constitution. Although the Emancipation Proclamation freed slaves in the Confederacy, the only way to guarantee permanent freedom for everyone was to amend the Constitution to abolish slavery.

On the History Matters website, read an interview with former slave Henry Blake. In what ways was life as a sharecropper similar to life as a slave?

 History Matters Henry Blake

RATION OF TRUTH

Historian Shelby Foote said that before the Civil War, people used the phrase the "United States are." After the war, people used the phrase the "United States is." No longer a collection of parts, the country was one whole.

In early 1864, Congress debated such an amendment. The amendment would only end slavery, not achieve racial equality.

The amendment needed two-thirds of the votes in both houses to become law. When Lincoln was reelected in November 1864, he used all his presidential power to convince Congress to vote for it. His efforts paid off. The amendment passed.

> The Thirteenth Amendment was sent to the states for ratification and, finally, on December 6, 1865, slavery was abolished throughout the United States.

The Thirteenth Amendment was just the start. The Civil Rights Act of 1866 declared everyone born in the United States (except Native Americans) a citizen. Johnson vetoed this act, claiming it violated states' rights. Congress overrode his veto, a first in American history.

In 1867, Congress also adopted a new Reconstruction plan. The South was divided into five military districts. Federal troops were sent in to maintain order. These troops would not leave, nor would a state be readmitted to the Union, until it ratified the Fourteenth Amendment, disqualified former Confederate officials from holding office, and granted suffrage to black men. The Fourteenth Amendment granted all citizens equal protection under the law.

President Johnson accused Republicans of trying to incite racial violence and tried to obstruct their Reconstruction efforts. In February 1868, the House of Representatives voted to impeach Johnson for resisting laws of Congress.

THE FIRST BLACK SENATOR

On February 25, 1870, Hiram Rhodes Revels (1827–1901) was sworn in as U.S. senator for the state of Mississippi, becoming the first African-American congressman in history. Jefferson Davis had previously held this seat. In debate prior to the ceremony, a senator from Maryland argued that Revels could not be a senator because he had not been a citizen for the nine years required by the constitution. The Maryland senator was technically correct, but only because blacks were not considered citizens until the Fourteenth was passed in 1868. But this man's views were in the minority. Revels took the oath and spectators in the gallery rose and watched the historic moment in silence.

President Grant's inauguration in 1869

credit: National Archives

Look at this map of the 1868 congressional elections. Based on the turnout for Republicans, what states had the highest concentration of African-American voters?

 rise of the black vote 1868

The Senate acquitted him by only one vote. Johnson remained in office, but for the rest of his presidency, he had no political power.

In 1868, Ulysses S. Grant was elected president, in part due to the support of blacks. At this time, only eight Northern states allowed African Americans to vote. Recognizing that freedom was incomplete without the right to vote, Congress passed the Fifteenth Amendment. This law declared that no state could deprive a citizen of the right to vote because of race or for having once been a slave.

More than 700,000 black men in the former Confederacy registered to vote. Almost 1,500 blacks were elected to political office.

South Carolina, Mississippi, and Louisiana had black constables and sheriffs, black judges and jurors. Sixteen blacks were elected to the U.S. Congress, nine of whom had been born slaves. The change was radical, but short-lived.

DEATH OF RECONSTRUCTION

Reconstruction died in 1877. Fear helped kill it. The Ku Klux Klan, a terrorist organization founded in Tennessee in 1865, unleashed a reign of terror in the late 1860s against blacks and their white allies. Violence and murder kept African Americans from exercising their newfound rights. The passage of the Ku Klux Klan Act in 1871 did lead to prosecution of Klan leaders and the organization was broken. However, the U.S. Supreme Court declared the Ku Klux Klan Act unconstitutional in 1882, and the terrorist group reemerged in the early twentieth century, stronger than ever.

To reassert white control, Southern officials found ways around the Fifteenth Amendment. Many states required African Americans to pass a literacy test before they could vote. Others charged a poll tax.

When blacks filed suit against this discrimination, the conservative Supreme Court interpreted the Fourteenth and Fifteenth Amendments to benefit the Southern states. Without the high court on its side, the federal government could not enforce voting rights or prosecute the Klan for violence.

The final blow to Reconstruction came in 1877. In the 1876 presidential election, Republican candidate Rutherford B. Hayes tied with the Democratic governor of New York. Democrats and Republicans made a secret deal that became known as the "Corrupt Bargain."

THE SECOND RECONSTRUCTION

In the 1950s, the modern civil rights movement challenged race relations across the country. With lawsuits, bus boycotts, sit-ins, and marches, African Americans fought for their rights. They battled state troopers, attack dogs, fire hoses, and assassins' bullets as they kept their eyes on the prize of equality. Gains came slowly, but they came, including integrated schools, a ban on discrimination in public accommodations, the right to vote. This "Second Reconstruction" achieved important victories for African Americans, although the United States still has a long way to go before true racial equality is achieved.

timeline
Confederate
monuments

WHOSE HISTORY?

In 2017, the United States had at least 1,503 monuments, statues, or places named for Confederate leaders. A grassroots effort to remove or rename these symbols has caused great controversy. Those who want the Confederate images to remain in place argue they celebrate Southern heritage—not hate—and removing such names and monuments amounts to erasing history. Critics insist these Confederate symbols ignore the heritage of the millions of African Americans whose ancestors were slaves and that the Confederacy was founded to preserve slavery.

Most Confederacy images were put in place decades after the Civil War. What events were going on then and why might these events have resulted in a move to resurrect the Confederacy?

Democrats agreed to accept Hayes as president and Republicans agreed to withdraw federal troops from the South. Southern blacks were at the mercy of whites who were eager to turn the clock back.

African-American participation in democracy dwindled year after year as Southern blacks were either prevented from voting or made too afraid to try. In Louisiana, the number of black voters dropped from 130,000 during Reconstruction to 5,000 by the end of the nineteenth century. A similar pattern occurred throughout the former Confederacy. As voting declined, so did black social and economic power.

> It would take another century and a civil rights revolution before African Americans would achieve the rights for which so many had died.

LESSONS LEARNED

Sam Watkins seemed content to leave the Civil War in the past. "The tale is told," Watkins wrote in his memoirs. "The world moves on . . . the blue dome of the sky sparkles with the trembling stars that twinkle and shine . . . and the scene melts and gradually disappears forever." Soldiers such as Sam Watkins and Elisha Hunt Rhodes might have died long ago, but the Civil War should not be confined to the dust bin of history. It still matters.

The Civil War revolutionized the way citizens perceived liberty and power. Union armies freed millions of enslaved people, proving the federal government could be liberty's savior. A national army was formed. A draft was imposed.

A national banking system was developed and new institutions, such as the Freedmen's Bureau, were created. While the Bill of Rights limited the power of the federal government, the Thirteenth, Fourteenth, and Fifteenth Amendments restricted the power of states in order to promote the welfare of all citizens. Union victory proved the federal government was supreme. While states still disagree with federal laws, politicians no longer threaten secession as a negotiating tool.

The Civil War offers a cautionary tale to modern Americans wrestling with controversial issues. Today, regional rivalries split the nation into red states and blue states. Americans argue over race and citizenship. States demand more freedom from the federal government. The Civil War shows what can happen when political passions blind people to compromise.

The Civil War also inspires. Although the nation paid a huge price in blood and treasure, slavery was destroyed. The war brought the nation further down the road toward the society dreamed of in 1776 where "all Men are created equal . . . and endowed [with] Life, Liberty and the Pursuit of Happiness." Sam Watkins penned history worth remembering when he wrote, "We are one and undivided."

VOCAB LAB

Write down what you think each word means. What root words can you find to help you? What does the context of the word tell you?

bigotry, **civil rights**, **economy**, **equality**, **impeach**, **integrate**, **literacy**, **oath**, **ratify**, **Reconstruction**, **sharecroppers**, **suffrage**, **vagrancy**, and **veteran**.

Compare your definitions with those of your friends or classmates. Did you all come up with the same meanings? Turn to the text and glossary if you need help.

KEY QUESTIONS

- **How might today's country be different if Reconstruction had continued in the 1800s?**
- **What parallels can you find between the United States of Civil War time and the United States today? What is different about the two periods?**

LEND A HAND

The bullet used in the Civil War, the minié ball, was made of soft lead that expanded when fired. Injuries caused by the minié ball often led to amputation of an arm or leg. Amputation was the safest, quickest, most effective means of saving a soldier's life, but the artificial limbs of the nineteenth century were clumsy and uncomfortable. Use common materials to design a light, flexible artificial hand.

- **Study your hand.** Note the movement of joints, muscles, and tendons. Research the anatomy of a human hand.

- **Create the design requirements of your artificial hand.** Must it look human-like? Be proportional? Be able to grip?

- **Construct and test your prototype.** Did the final product meet your requirements? If not, how can you redesign the hand to meet your goals?

Suggested Supplies ▼

- objects to use for fingers, such as plastic straws, PVC piping, rubber gloves, popsicle sticks, or irrigation tubing

- material for tendons, such as string, rubber bands, or metal wire

- material to serve as the hand, such as polymer clay, a block of wood with holes drilled in it, or a cardboard tube

- "skin" to hold the parts of the hand together, such as a hot glue gun or duct tape

> **To investigate more,** redesign your hand with more or fewer fingers or with different materials. How do these changes impact the effectiveness of the hand? Go to the U.S. Library of Medicine's online exhibit, titled "Life and Limb," to learn more about amputations during the Civil War. What factors determined whether a soldier survived an amputation?

 Life and Limb

BIO POEM—WHO AM I?

Wars are fueled by misunderstanding. When people do not take the time to understand each other's backgrounds, hopes, or fears, conflicts escalate quickly. Write a bio poem so people can learn the real you, deep inside.

- **List characteristics that describe you.** Think deeply about experiences, hopes, fears, and accomplishments that have shaped your identity.

- **Write a bio poem that follows this 11-line structure and answers the question, "Who am I?"**

    Line 1: First name

    Line 2: Four adjectives describing you

    Line 3: Discuss a relationship

    Line 4: Three things you love

    Line 5: Three feelings

    Line 6: Three needs

    Line 7: Three gifts

    Line 8: Three fears

    Line 9: Three experiences you want to have

    Line 10: Where you live

    Line 11: Last name

- **Exchange bio poems with a friend.** As you read, jot down questions or comments in the margin of their work. Talk about your poems after reading.

To investigate more, write a bio poem about someone involved in the Civil War or write two bio poems, one about someone from the Union and one about someone from the Confederacy. How can understanding people deeply help resolve conflict?

GLOSSARY

abolitionist: a person who wants to end slavery.

abomination: something that causes hatred or disgust.

accomplice: a person who helps someone commit a crime.

acquit: to find someone not guilty of a charge.

activism: working to create social change.

activist: a person who fights for something they believe in.

agitate: to stir up or disturb.

alienate: to cause someone to feel isolated.

alleged: to declare that something has occurred without proof.

alliance: a partnership between peoples or countries.

ambitious: a strong desire to succeed.

amendment: a change or addition to a motion, bill, or constitution.

amputation: when a surgeon cuts off a limb.

annihilate: totally destroy.

anthem: a song praising and declaring loyalty to something or a popular song that has become associated with a group, period, or cause that celebrates a sense of solidarity.

appeal: to make an urgent request.

appointment: to assign someone a specific job or position.

armory: a storage place for weapons and other war equipment.

arsenal: a place where weapons or military equipment are stored and manufactured.

artillery: large guns such as cannon and howitzers.

assassinate: to murder a person, usually for political reasons.

avert: to prevent something from happening.

backlash: a strong negative reaction.

ban: to prevent by law.

barrage: to bombard someone.

battery: a collection of artillery in an offensive or defensive position.

bigotry: intolerance for anyone with a different religion, race, or belief system.

billet: to sleep somewhere, in a nonmilitary place.

biopoem: a simple poem about a person that follows a certain pattern.

blockade: closing off a place or port to prevent entry or exit.

bluff: a steep cliff.

bondage: being enslaved.

boycott: to refuse to buy certain goods or use certain services as a form of protest.

brigade: a subdivision of an army.

brutal: very unpleasant or difficult.

bummer: a forager.

burden: a heavy load.

canteen: a water bottle used by soldiers.

cargo: a load carried on a ship or aircraft.

carnage: the killing of many people.

casualty: someone killed or injured in battle.

cauldron: a situation of instability and strong emotion.

cavalry: an army of soldiers on horseback.

census: an official count or survey of a population that records various details about individuals.

chasm: a deep crack or hole.

circuit: a loop that starts and finishes at the same place.

circumvent: to find a way around an obstacle.

citizen: a legally recognized subject of a country.

civil rights: the rights granted to citizens of a country.

civil war: a war between citizens of the same nation.

colonist: a settler.

colonization: when a group of people settle in a new place, taking control of it and eventually calling it their own.

commission: a directive or assignment of an officer in the military.

commissioned: the act of entrusting someone with certain power and authority.

commissioner: a person in charge of a certain department or district.

company: a military unit under the command of a captain.

comprehensive: complete.

compromise: an agreement reached by two sides working together.

concession: to give in on a demand.

concise: to give a lot of information clearly and in a few words.

condemnation: strong disapproval.

confederacy: a group of people, states, or nations that comes together for a common purpose. The Confederacy refers to the group of Southern slave states that seceded from the Union and formed its own government in 1861.

Confederate States of America: the nation formed by 11 states that seceded from the United States.

confiscate: when someone in authority seizes a possession.

conspirator: a person involved in a secret plan to do harm.

constitution: a written set of basic principles and laws by which a nation is governed.

contraband: slaves that escaped or were brought to Union lines.

controversial: likely to cause the public to disagree and argue over something.

convention: a gathering of people who are all interested in a certain idea, topic, or event.

convict: to find someone guilty of a crime.

customs agent: a government official who collects taxes on imports and exports.

daguerreotype: an early form of a photograph.

death knell: refers to something soon to be destroyed or soon to fail.

debate: a discussion between people with differing viewpoints.

decisive: to make decisions quickly.

decree: an official order.

delegate: someone who goes to a meeting to represent his or her city or country.

demoralized: to lose confidence or hope.

desertion: when a soldier is absent from his military post without authorization.

diplomat: a person sent by the government to deal with another country.

dire: a serious situation.

disband: to break up or dissolve an organization.

discrimination: the unfair treatment of a person or a group of people because of their identity.

disembark: to get off a vehicle.

draft: a requirement to serve in the military.

economy: the wealth and resources of an area or country.

electoral vote: a vote cast by a member of the Electoral College, which determines the winner of the president and vice president in the United States.

elite: people with the most wealth or the highest status.

enlist: to enroll in the military.

emancipate: to free.

embed: to fix firmly into something.

emigration: to leave one's own country to settle in another.

equality: to be treated the same.

erosion: the process by which surface soil and rock are worn away.

escalate: to increase rapidly or get worse.

evacuate: to leave a dangerous place to go to a safe place.

explicitly: very clearly.

export: to send goods to another country for sale.

fanatically: extremely and irrationally enthusiastic.

fatigue: exhaustion, tiredness.

federal: related to the central government.

federalism: the system of government in which the states share power with the federal government.

Federals: soldiers of the Union Army.

flamboyant: excessively showy.

flotilla: fleet of ships or boats.

flourish: to grow vigorously.

foe: an enemy.

forager: a person who searches for food or other provisions, often from the natural world.

forbade: to not allow.

foretold: to have predicted something.

fortification: a walled-in area to protect against an enemy.

fugitive: a runaway slave.

Fugitive Slave Law: an 1850 law that required all citizens of the United States to aid in the capture of runaway slaves.

gallant: brave or heroic.

galled: to make someone feel annoyed.

gangly: tall, thin, and awkward.

gangrene: an infection that kills body tissue.

garrison: a military post where troops are stationed.

guerrilla warfare: hit-and-run attacks by small groups of fighters who are not members of a regular army.

GLOSSARY

gunboat: foreign policy backed up by the use or threat of military force.

hamper: to restrict or hinder.

hardtack: a hard biscuit that was part of a soldier's ration.

haversack: a soldier's knapsack.

hearing: a special session of Congress held to "hear" from witnesses and experts on a given issue.

hindsight: an understanding of a situation only after it has already occurred.

hostility: negative or angry feelings.

House of Representatives: the lower house of the U.S. Congress.

humane: to show compassion and kindness.

immigrant: a person who comes to live in another country.

impeach: to charge an elected official with misconduct.

impenetrable: impossible to break into.

import: to bring in goods from another country in order to sell them.

importation: the act of bringing in any good or service from another country.

impregnable: unable to be captured or broken into.

inauguration: a ceremony or celebration to introduce a person or thing.

incentive: the possibility of a reward that encourages people to do something or work harder.

indiscriminately: in a way that does not show care or judgment.

industrialize: to change from manufacturing goods by hand to producing products in factories.

ineffective: something that does not produce the desired result.

infamous: well known because of something bad.

injustice: unfair action or treatment.

institution: an established practice or custom.

insurrection: a rebellion or revolt.

integrate: to become part of.

ironclad: a type of armored plating on nineteenth-century warships.

justice: fair treatment.

justify: to show or prove that something is right or reasonable.

lame duck: a president in the last few months of his term after his successor has been elected.

liberty: to be free from unfair or overly restrictive rules imposed by authority.

literacy: the ability to read and write.

manifest: a document listing the cargo, passengers, and crew of a ship.

martyr: a person who endures great suffering and death for his or her beliefs.

massacre: to deliberately kill a large number of people.

mass-produce: to manufacture large amounts of a product.

migraine: a terrible headache.

militia: a group of citizens who are trained to fight but who only serve in time of emergency.

Missouri Compromise: the 1820 law that admitted Missouri into the Union as a slave state.

moral: relating to right and wrong behavior and character.

morale: feelings of enthusiasm and loyalty that a person or group has about a task or job.

muster out: to discharge from military service.

negotiate: to reach an agreement, compromise, or treaty through bargaining and discussing.

null and void: to cancel or make invalid.

oath: a solemn promise.

obstruct: to block.

offensive: an attacking military campaign.

opponent: the person or group against which a person is fighting.

ordinance: an order or decree.

pacify: to calm down.

pamphlet: a small booklet or leaflet.

pallor: an unhealthy, pale appearance.

paralysis: when you're unable to move.

pardon: to forgive.

parliament: the law-making body of the British government.

parole: to release a prisoner before their sentence is completed.

patriot: a person who vigorously supports their country.

permanent: intending to last forever.

persevere: to not give up.

persona: the aspect of someone's character seen by others.

petition: a collection of signatures, signed by a group of people, requesting that a change be made.

pillage: to violently rob during wartime.

pivotal: vitally important.

plantation: a large farm on which crops are grown for sale at market.

platform: the principles on which a political party campaigns.

political party: an organized group of people with similar political goals and opinions.

politician: someone who is either a holder or a candidate for elected office.

poll: the process of voting in an election or to record the opinion of people on an issue.

POW: prisoner of war.

precede: to come before.

premature: early.

principle: an important idea or belief that guides an individual or community.

proclamation: a public announcement.

prolonged: when something is lengthened, or lasts longer that it was supposed to.

propaganda: information designed to persuade people to believe a certain political view. The information is often biased or misleading.

prototype: a preliminary model.

purge: to get rid of, move, or eliminate something.

Quaker: a member of a Christian religious movement.

race: a group of people of common ancestry who share certain physical characteristics such as skin color.

racial: something related to how people are divided on the basis of shared physical characteristics.

radical: extreme, or a person with extreme political or social views.

rallied: called together for a common goal.

ransack: to search for something in a way that causes damage or makes a mess.

ratify: to give official approval of something, such as a constitutional amendment.

ration: an amount of food or water allowed per day in order to make the food or water last as long as possible.

rebel: to fight against authority or a person who fights against authority.

rebel yell: the battle cry used by Confederate soldiers.

rebellion: to openly resist authority.

Rebels: soldiers in the Confederate Army.

Reconstruction: the period after the Civil War in which the seceded states were brought back into the United States.

recruit: to get someone to join you or help you. Also a person who joins.

refugee: a person forced to leave his or her native land to seek safety, usually as a result of war or persecution.

reinforcements: more troops.

relentless: unwilling to give up.

religious conviction: a strong religious belief.

relocation: to be moved to a different place.

renege: to go back on your word, to not do what you said you were going to do.

repel: to push away or apart.

representative: a single person who speaks for the wishes of a group.

reprieve: a short time of relief.

republic: a government in which citizens exercise power through elected representatives.

resolution: a firm decision to do or not do something.

revile: to criticize someone in a very hostile way.

revolution: a dramatic, widespread change in society.

revolutionary: someone committed to fighting a ruler or political system.

roughshod: messy.

ruffian: a violent person.

safeguard: to protect.

sanctuary: a place of refuge or safety.

scurvy: a disease caused by a diet lacking in vitamin C.

secede: to formally withdraw from a country.

sharecropper: a farmer who works someone else's land and gives a portion of their crop as rent.

sharpshooter: someone very skilled at shooting guns.

shorthand: a way of taking notes using abbreviations.

GLOSSARY

siege: when the military surrounds a town or enemy fort and does not allow anything in or out.

skeptical: suspicious.

skirmish: a brief fight between two groups.

slave: a person owned by another person and forced to work, without pay, against his or her will.

slavery: when slaves are used as workers.

smuggle: to move goods illegally in or out of a country.

socialite: a person well known in high-class society.

spire: a pointy structure that decorates the top of a building.

stalemate: a contest where neither side is winning.

states' rights: the rights and powers held by individual states, not the federal government.

stenographer: a person who transcribes a speech into shorthand.

stockade: a solid fence made with strong posts standing upright in the ground.

stockpile: to store large amounts of something for later use. Also called hoarding.

strategic: carefully designed to serve a particular purpose.

strife: disagreement.

suffrage: the right to vote.

sulfurous: smoky and smelling of sulfur.

suppress: to prevent an event from happening.

surplus: an extra supply of something.

surrender: to give up or give something over to an enemy.

tactics: a carefully planned action or strategy to achieve something.

tariff: a tax on imported goods.

tarnish: to stain or dirty.

tax: an extra fee the government charges on certain products.

technology: the tools, methods, and systems used to solve a problem or do work.

telegraph: a device for tapping out coded messages over wires using electrical signals.

terrorist: a person who uses violence and threats to frighten people.

textile: cloth or fabric.

thesis: a sentence that summarizes a main claim developed from research.

Three-Fifths Compromise: an agreement reached in 1787 that allowed slave states to count each slave as three-fifths of a person for determining how many representatives each state had in Congress.

torrential: flowing intensely in large quantities.

total war strategy: the destruction of any resource that will help an enemy.

trade: to buy and sell goods and services.

traitor: someone who betrays their country.

transatlantic slave trade: the international system of trade in which kidnapped Africans were transported across the Atlantic and sold as slaves.

transcribe: to write down.

traumatize: to cause lasting shock because of emotional or physical injury.

treason: actions that go against one's own country.

troops: soldiers or armed forces.

tyranny: cruel or oppressive government.

Underground Railroad: a network of houses and safe places that runaway slaves went to, from one to the next, on the way north to freedom.

Union: the term used for the federal (national) government of the United States in the Civil War, which also referred to the Northern states.

unity: togetherness.

U.S. Senate: a law-making body in the United States federal government.

vagrancy: the state of living as a vagrant. Homelessness.

veteran: a former soldier.

veto: to reject a law or policy.

vigilante: someone who takes the law into his own hands.

volley: many bullets fired at once.

wince: a shrinking movement of the body out of or in anticipation of pain or distress.

writ of habeas corpus: a court order requiring law enforcement to bring an arrested person before a judge and explain the reason for the person's detention to determine if it is legal.

Yankee: a person who lives in, or is from, the United States. During the Civil War, it referred to an inhabitant of New England or one of the Northern states.

SELECTED BIBLIOGRAPHY

Foote, Shelby. *The Civil War: A Narrative—Fort Sumter to Perryville*. New York: Vintage Books, 1986.

Foote, Shelby. *The Civil War: A Narrative—Fredericksburg to Meridian*. New York: Random House, 1963.

Foote, Shelby. *The Civil War: A Narrative—Red River to Appomattox*. New York: Random House, 1974.

Jones, Wilmer L. *Generals in Blue and Gray: Lincoln's Generals*.
Volume I. Westport, Connecticut: Praeger, 2004. 171.

McPherson, James. *Battle Cry of Freedom*. New York: Oxford University Press, 1988.

Rhodes, Elisha Hunt. *All For the Union: The Civil War Diary and Letters of Elisha Hunt
Rhodes*. Ed. Robert Hunt Rhodes. New York: Orion, 1985.

Ward, Geoffrey C., Ken Burns, and Ric Burns. *The Civil War: An
Illustrated History*. New York: Alfred A. Knopf, 1990.

Watkins, Sam R. *Co. Aytch: A Confederate Memoir of the Civil War*. New York: Simon & Schuster, 1962.

Wheeler, Richard. *Voices of the Civil War*. New York: Meridian, 1976.

Wiley, Bell I. *The Life of Johnny Reb and the Life of Billy Yank*. NY: Essential Classics of the Civil War. 1994.

NONFICTION FOR YOUNG READERS

Armstrong, Jennifer. *Photo by Brady: A Picture of the Civil War*. New York: Atheneum, 2005.

Bolden, Tonya. *Emancipation Proclamation: Lincoln and the Dawn of Liberty*. New York: Abrams, 2013.

Freedman, Russell. *Abraham Lincoln and Frederick Douglass: The Story
Behind an American Friendship*. New York: Clarion Books, 2012.

Murphy, Jim. *The Boys' War: Confederate and Union Soldiers Talk
About the Civil War*. New York: Clarion Books, 1990.

Shaara, Michael. *The Killer Angels:The Classic Novel of the Civil War*. New York: Ballantine, 1974.

CIVIL WAR WEBSITES

Africans in America. pbs.org/wgbh/aia/part4/title.html

This website takes the viewer through the experience of African Americans from slavery through the Civil War.

The Civil War Home Page. civil-war.net

This site is a digital collection of thousands of maps, images, letters, and
other documents that recount the story of the Civil War.

Civil War Trust. civilwar.org/education/students

The Civil War Trust is a nonprofit organization dedicated to preserving Civil War battlefields. Its website contains a wealth of information about the war, including maps, primary sources, and interviews with experts.

RESOURCES

HISTORIC SITES

Andersonville National Historic Site: Located in Andersonville, Georgia, this park is the site of the notorious Confederate prison camp and also houses a national cemetery and the National Prisoner of War Museum.

Fort Sumter National Monument, Charleston, South Carolina: Tour the remains of the fort where the Civil War began.

Gettysburg National Military Park: Located in Gettysburg, Pennsylvania, this park has a visitors' center that contains a museum of the battle, as well as a national cemetery and 6,000 acres of battlefield to explore.

Harper's Ferry National Historical Park: This park is situated where the Potomac and Shenandoah Rivers meet in West Virginia. Step back in time and enter the historic town of Harper's Ferry and walk in the footsteps of radical abolitionist John Brown.

SOURCE NOTES

INTRODUCTION

1 Watkins, Sam R. *Co. Aytch: A Confederate Memoir of the Civil War*. New York: Simon & Schuster, 1962.

2 Rhodes, Elisha Hunt. *All For the Union: The Civil War Diary and Letters of Elisha Hunt Rhodes*. Ed. Robert Hunt Rhodes. New York: Orion, 1985.

CHAPTER 1

1 Lubet, Steven. *Fugitive Justice: Runaways, Rescuers, and Slavery on Trial*. Cambridge, MA: Harvard University Press, 2010. 157.

2 "Bleeding Kansas." *Africans in America*. PBS, n.d. Web. 7 Jan. 2013.

3 Foote, Shelby. *The Civil War: A Narrative—Fort Sumter to Perryville*. New York: Vintage Books, 1986.

CHAPTER 2

1 Lincoln, Abraham. "House Divided Speech." *Africans in America*. PBS, n.d. Web. 4 April 2017. www.pbs.org/wgbh/aia/part4/4h2934t.html.

CHAPTER 3

1 Rhodes, Elisha Hunt. *All For the Union: The Civil War Diary and Letters of Elisha Hunt Rhodes*. Ed. Robert Hunt Rhodes. New York: Orion, 1985.

2 Lineberry, Cate. "The Wild Rose of Washington." *The New York Times*. The New York Times, 22 Aug. 2011. Web. 09 March 2017.

CHAPTER 4

1 "Gunboat Defeat on Valentine's Day." *History E-Library*. National Park Service, n.d. Web. 14 March 2017.

2 Foote, Shelby. *The Civil War: A Narrative—Fort Sumter to Perryville*. New York: Vintage Books, 1986.

3 Ward, Geoffrey C., Ken Burns, and Ric Burns. *The Civil War: An Illustrated History*. New York: Alfred A. Knopf, 1990.

CHAPTER 5

1 Lincoln, Abraham. "Fifth Debate: Galesburg, Illinois." Lincoln Home. National Park Service, n.d. Web. 11 April 2017. www.nps.gov/liho/learn/historyculture/debate5.htm.

2 Masur, Louis P. *Lincoln's Hundred Days: The Emancipation Proclamation and the War for the Union*. Cambridge, MA: Harvard University Press, 2012.

3 Klingaman, William K. *Abraham Lincoln and the Road to Emancipation: 1861–1865*. New York: Viking, 2001.

CHAPTER 6

1 Schulte, Brigid. "Women soldiers fought, bled and died in the Civil War, then were forgotten." *The Washington Post*. The Washington Post, 29 April 2013. Web. 16 March 2017. www.washingtonpost.com/local/women-soldiers-fought-bled-and-died-in-the-civ....

2 *The Confederate Veteran Magazine*. Vol. II. January 1894-December 1894. Willington: Broadfoot Publishing.

3 Mitchell, Robert M. "Sherman's March to the Sea: A military triumph left a bitter legacy." *The Washington Post*. The Washington Post, 13 Sept. 2014. Web. 25 March 2017.

4 Flood, Charles Bracelen. *Grant and Sherman: The Friendship that Won the Civil War*. New York: Farrar, Straus and Giroux, 2005.

CHAPTER 7

1 Foote, Shelby. *The Civil War: A Narrative—Red River to Appomattox*. New York: Random House, 1974.

2 McPherson, James. *Battle Cry of Freedom*. New York: Oxford University Press, 1988.

CHAPTER 8

1 Brundage, W. Fitzhugh. "Reconstruction and the Formerly Enslaved." Teacher Serve. National Humanities Center, n.d. Web. 29 March 2017.

QR CODE GLOSSARY

Page 6: leventhalmap.org/id/14382

Page 11: gutenberg.org/ebooks/203?msg=welcome_stranger

Page 11: nps.gov/jame/learn/historyculture/african-americans-at-jamestown.htm

Page 12: inmotionaame.org/gallery/detail.cfm;jsessionid=f8301137001491173 401439?migration=1&topic=8&id=1_006M&type=map&bhcp=1

Page 13: pbs.org/wgbh/aia/part3/3narr6.html

Page 14: teachingamericanhistory.org/static/neh/interactives/sectionalism/lesson1

Page 20: slavevoyages.org

Page 23: nps.gov/liho/learn/historyculture/debates.htm

Page 26: jeffersondavis.rice.edu/archives/documents/jefferson-davis-reply-senate-william-h-seward

Page 28: avalon.law.yale.edu/19th_century/csa_csainau.asp

Page 28: abrahamlincolnonline.org/lincoln/speeches/1inaug.htm

Page 29: civilwar.org

Page 31: dsl.richmond.edu/voting/presvoting.html

RESOURCES

Page 32: civil-war.net/pages/ordinances_secession.asp

Page 37: sonofthesouth.net/leefoundation/civil-war/1861/august/early-bull-run.htm

Page 39: pbs.org/kenburns/civil-war/war/maps/#/detail/unions-grand-strategy

Page 40: rbscp.lib.rochester.edu/4373

Page 44: civilwarheritagetrails.org/civil-war-music/battle-cry-of-freedom.html

Page 48: docsouth.unc.edu/neh/keckley/keckley.html

Page 52: civilwar.org/learn/maps/shiloh-animated-map?referrer=https%3A//www.google.com

Page 56: nps.gov/media/photo/gallery.htm?id=2412F92B-1DD8-B71C-0728A9DF066D2649

Page 58: learnmorsecode.com

Page 61: teachingamericanhistory.org/library/document/the-slaveholders-rebellion

Page 63: dsl.richmond.edu/emancipation

Page 67: smithsonianmag.com/history/A-Cutting-Edge-Second-Look-at-the-Battle-of-Gettysburg-1-180947921

Page 69: avalon.law.yale.edu/19th_century/gettyb.asp

Page 70: loc.gov/collections/civil-war-maps/?fa=subject%3Agettysburg

Page 70: civilwar.org/learn/maps/gettysburg-campaign-map

Page 72: loc.gov/exhibits/civil-war-in-america/april-1861-april-1862.html

Page 72: gilderlehrman.org/mweb/search?needle=civil%20war%20recruitment%20posters

Page 77: washingtonpost.com/local/women-soldiers-fought-bled-and-died-in-the-civil-war-then-were-forgotten/2013/04/26/fa722dba-a1a2-11e2-82bc-511538ae90a4_story.html?utm_term=.297c3eca62d1

Page 78: loc.gov/pictures/resource/ppmsca.09326

Page 80: loc.gov/pictures/resource/ppmsca.09326

Page 85: nps.gov/media/photo/gallery.htm?id=25001AB0-1DD8-B71C-079A07B44D6707A4

Page 89: jeffersondavis.rice.edu/archives/documents/list-documents-available-online

Page 91: indiana.edu/~liblilly/history/history3.html

Page 93: killinglincoln.nationalgeographic.com

Page 96: loc.gov/item/gvhs01.vhs00179

Page 99: www.digitalhistory.uh.edu/exhibits/reconstruction/section2/section2_family.html

Page 100: digital.nypl.org/schomburg/images_aa19/reconst.cfm

Page 102: historymatters.gmu.edu/d/6377

Page 104: umich.edu/~lawrace/votetour2.htm

Page 106: splcenter.org/sites/default/files/whoseheritage_splc.pdf

Page 108: nlm.nih.gov/exhibition/lifeandlimb

INDEX